Living with PTSD on the Autism Spectrum

by the same authors

Living Through Suicide Loss with an Autistic Spectrum Disorder (ASD)
An Insider Guide for Individuals, Family, Friends, and Professional Responders
Lisa Morgan, M.Ed.
ISBN 978 1 78592 729 4
eISBN 978 1 78450 400 7

Spectrum Women—Autism and Parenting
Renata Jurkevythz, Maura Campbell and Lisa Morgan
ISBN 978 1 78775 294 8
eISBN 978 1 78775 295 5

Spectrum Women
Walking to the Beat of Autism
Edited by Barb Cook and Dr Michelle Garnett
Foreword by Lisa Morgan
ISBN 978 1 78592 434 7
eISBN 978 1 78450 806 7

Living with PTSD on the Autism Spectrum

Insightful Analysis with Practical Applications

Lisa Morgan, M.Ed. and Mary P. Donahue, Ph.D.

Foreword by Tony Attwood

Jessica Kingsley Publishers
London and Philadelphia

First published in Great Britain in 2021 by Jessica Kingsley Publishers

An Hachette Company

2

Printed and bound by CPI Group (UK) Ltd, Croydon, CR0 4YY

Jessica Kingsley Publishers' policy is to use papers that are natural, renewable
and recyclable products and made from wood grown in sustainable forests. The
logging and manufacturing processes are expected to conform to the environmental
regulations of the country of origin.

Jessica Kingsley Publishers
73 Collier Street
London N1 9BE, UK

www.jkp.com

This book is dedicated to all autistic people with a dual diagnosis of post-traumatic stress disorder, and the mental health providers working with them.

It is our sincere hope that this book will serve as a tool to communicate and understand the unique manifestations of symptoms and difficulties surrounding this affliction.

Contents

Disclaimer

With respect to all the different ways people diagnosed with an autism spectrum disorder can describe themselves in print, we have chosen to use identity first language in our book. We also use the terms: ASD, autistic, non-autistic, neurotypical, NT, and neurodivergent throughout the book as needed to maintain the meaning and flow of the text.

Autism is known as a spectrum condition. We recognize the individuality of all autistic people and understand the shared lived experiences will not resonate with everyone. The book is autism friendly and we believe there are enough situations and circumstances covered to benefit all autistic people, as well as professionals, family, and friends.

This book features both personal and professional experience backed up by best practice research. We have shared parts of our lives in the hope of bringing awareness of living with the dual diagnosis of an autism spectrum/post-traumatic stress disorder. This book is in no way endorsing any particular type of professional mental health therapies or interventions.

Always, without exception, seek out the advice of your mental health provider or other qualified professionals if you need help or have any questions regarding your well-being.

Foreword

Those who have autism live in a world that creates high levels of stress and anxiety for them. They feel confused and overwhelmed by social and sensory experiences, and have considerable difficulty accessing, regulating and communicating their emotions. Their developmental history may also include being rejected and abused by peers since early childhood, leading to a sense of loneliness and depression. In the adult years, the person may be greatly stressed by not obtaining the academic, relationship and employment success that might have been expected, considering their intellectual abilities; and often there is a continuation of experiences that are perceived as traumatizing.

The high levels of stress and anxiety can make the person overly sensitive and reactive to aversive events, causing hypervigilance, low resilience and an amplification of the depth of emotional response. The level of emotional trauma and stress due to specific, and often repeated, experiences can lead to the diagnosis of post-traumatic stress disorder (PTSD). In my extensive clinical experience, I have seen many children, adolescents and adults at all levels of expression of autism, with an additional diagnosis of PTSD.

Clinicians need to review a person's developmental history and current circumstances in order to screen for PTSD and recognize that some behaviors that appear to be almost random may be PTSD flashbacks and panic attacks. PTSD will also increase the signs and expression of autism, thus having a negative impact on social engagement and reciprocity, and the ability to read someone's intentions; and there may be an accentuation of the need to maintain sameness for safety, heightened sensory sensitivity, and an increased desire to pursue interests to act as a thought blocker.

The origins of PTSD can be due to experiences at home and school, as well as those in government institutions, such as psychiatric wards or prisons. The key factor is the person's perception of a given event and subsequent trauma. Added to this is the autistic characteristic of having difficulty determining whether an action was, in fact, malicious or accidental, along with a tendency to ruminate on why someone would engage in the behavior that led to the trauma.

A typical person would be able to disclose their inner thoughts and feelings related to their experiences of trauma, with a natural eloquence and vocabulary to describe subtle and intense emotions. However, those who have autism have great difficulty converting thoughts and emotions into conversational speech. They also often do not want to communicate their suppressed feelings, as this would lead to re-experiencing the distress. They may be unsure that the other person would understand their emotional response to events that would not necessarily be perceived as traumatic by a typical person. Thus, conventional psychotherapy must accommodate the profile of abilities associated with autism in order to provide the necessary therapy for PTSD.

In my conversations with those who have autism, I frequently identify themes of trust and safety, social disconnection and a pervasive pessimism that their lives will always include traumatic experiences. They also identify a lack of literature on autism and PTSD. As I read the manuscript for *Living with PTSD on the Autism Spectrum: Insightful Analysis with Practical Applications*, I felt that, at last, we have a resource that will not only facilitate understanding from a personal and professional perspective, but will also change lives and lead to the effective treatment of PTSD in someone who has autism.

Professor Tony Attwood

Acknowledgments

The writing of this book has been an integral step in my journey towards healing. I could not have written this book without MaryD. She has supported me unabashedly and right up until the very minute we hit the "send" button, she reminded me that I had the freedom to walk away if it was too much out of my comfort zone.

My children are the joy of my life. My two oldest, Rachel and Ben, support me as adult friends. My two youngest, still living at home, Levi and Gabriel, have supported me by learning to cook, taking on more chores, and being patient while I spent so much time writing during the past two years.

And, the One who has always been with me in spirit when humans either couldn't or wouldn't. I have found out through the years of my life, there was no hurt so painful, no loneliness so heavy, and no darkness so absolute—that He wasn't deeper still, waiting for me with peace that surpasses all understanding.

Lisa

Thanks to my mighty support system; my siblings who offered advice and food at just the right time. To those who courageously allowed me to use their stories. To Patrick, thanks for the talks and for being typically forthright in our discussions. Pris and Liz, cuz you rock! And, of course, to my Seany, who encourages me in all my adventures. I'm a lucky girl.

MaryD

Proviso

This book was written from the perspective of two people who grew up and worked in the New England area of the USA. Though we have each traveled and lived in other cultures, our main developmental experiences were in the context of our respective rural towns and Puritanical exposure. In addition, the degree of access to services and providers has greatly influenced our individual views of this journey. Other cultural considerations such as low socioeconomic status, religious beliefs, gender, degree of education, family size, and social support should also be taken into account by the reader. Therefore, this book should be read as the specific journey of two people—one considered neurotypical and the other neurodivergent—who seek to understand each other for their own sakes and for greater goals. For Lisa, she sought relief from the intense and overwhelming feelings resulting from a lifetime of trauma. For MaryD, who regularly practices in the area of trauma and domestic violence, learning how to work with spectrum women was a natural progression. Together, they hope to begin an earnest dialogue about the underserved issues resulting from the occurrence of PTSD prevalent in the ASD population.

Preface

Do you know what happens when post-traumatic stress disorder (PTSD) and autism spectrum disorder (ASD) meet in the same unfortunate person? I do. A symbiotic relationship forms and the symptomology of PTSD is enhanced by certain inherent characteristics of autism creating a life marred by the struggles of a dual diagnosis that works with, and against, the other.

Let me explain what I mean.

PTSD flashbacks are triggered and experienced over and over again by a couple of defining characteristics of autism—perseveration and rumination.

PTSD nightmares are made more lucid by an autistic brain that thinks in pictures.

The emotions invoked by reliving trauma during flashbacks can create chaos in an autistic person who is not in touch with and/or does not understand their emotions. Strong emotions can become overwhelming quickly; and not knowing how to handle their emotions can cause an autistic meltdown leaving the autistic person in crisis.

PTSD panic attacks are exacerbated by the ever-present anxiety autistic people already live with and deepen the depression many autistic people suffer day after day.

Autistic people typically do not reach out to others for help, so an autistic person with PTSD can be very disconnected and alone using maladaptive coping skills.

The walk towards health and healing from PTSD can become

outrageously difficult, with the autism and PTSD working together to create a sense of overwhelming anxiety, panic, and chaos of thoughts.

In this book, I will share my experiences of living with PTSD and autism. MaryD will share her professional knowledge about the challenges of diagnosing PTSD in an autistic person, working with the unique communication differences, and describe her view of the symptomology of PTSD in an autistic person.

We will look at what research is available and show that research is gravely needed in the area of the connection between ASD and traumatic experiences, which may ultimately develop into PTSD.

The unique characteristics of ASD determine which events are experienced as particularly traumatic (e.g., social insults and degradation, sensory overstimulation, abrupt changes in known routines, pervasive aloneness) and affect both the manifestation and severity of PTSD among diagnosed individuals. It must be remembered that what may be traumatic for an autistic person will not necessarily be traumatic for a non-autistic person and can't be dismissed by anyone trying to help.

For example, difficulty with changes in the routine of an autistic person is a defining aspect of ASD listed in the *DSM-V* (APA 2013), yet I have reached out many times trying to explain how much a change has upset me, only to be told that "no one really likes change." It's not that I don't like it; it's more like my life seems ruined in the moment by a change in routine, no matter how big or small.

This book will also cover exploitative relationships and how autistic individuals are vulnerable to being involved in abusive relationships without recognizing the abuse or knowing how to escape it. This leaves autistic individuals susceptible to chronic relational trauma, which over time can develop into PTSD.

The autistic adult who does reach out for help and interacts with first responders, doctors, and victim advocates may find themselves traumatized due to the lack of understanding and communication difficulties between themselves and the people helping them, which is also a reason why many autistic adults do not reach out for help.

Finally, we will discuss the therapeutic relationship between an autistic individual and therapists, doctors, and other professionals. We will help you consider ways to build and keep trust, how to work through cultural competencies, which therapeutic model works best, and tips to help you get more out of therapy according to the neurological differences of ASD, such as perseveration, cognitive rigidity, social deficits, and sensory challenges.

This book is the go-to book on PTSD in autistic individuals for the layperson, clinicians, first responders, family, and friends, as well as for academia.

Lisa Morgan, M.Ed.

Chapter I

A History of ASD and PTSD

Co-occurring autism spectrum disorder and post-traumatic stress disorder: What do we know?

As with all sciences, psychology is imperfect. That's what makes it so exciting! There are always new ideas and subsequent discoveries. Mental health and knowledge of the mind is ever-evolving. Thanks to open-minded researchers and practitioners, people willing to open themselves up to skepticism and wonder, we now know that skull shape doesn't mean psychosis, and that the uterus doesn't float around the body. Each time a theory is disproved, more questions follow, leading in different directions. An idea occurs, it develops as the evidence takes it, and the idea turns into theory with more evidence, both scientific and practical, as it evolves into "best practice." This is, of course, how we know what we know...to date. It's important, however, not to forget where these ideas came from and how they evolved into what we know today—and how they inform the future. Thus, let's look individually at ASD and PTSD in terms of where we've been and where we are.

I. Autism
History of autism diagnosis

Though there are many accounts of individuals displaying symptomology related to ASD from as early as the 1800s, it was officially entered in the DSM (*Diagnostic and Statistical*

Manual of Mental Disorders) in 1980 (APA 1980). At that point, it was a disorder of childhood called "Infantile Autism," used as a means of differentiating it from schizophrenia. Work towards its diagnostic differentiation led to replacing the label with "Autistic Disorder" in 1987 and, in the early 1990s, to its being classified in the USA as a special education category. Thus, research on autism increased. Asperger's Syndrome (AS), considered at that time a milder form of ASD, was differentiated and added to the *DSM-IV* (APA 1994) in 1994. Subsequent research revealed autism to be a much more varied condition than initially considered. With a large number of criteria and so many different variations observed, it became clear that autism occurs on a spectrum rather than in specially defined and confined criteria. Rather than maintaining primary criteria and sub-diagnoses, the newest version of the DSM (*DSM-V*; APA 2013) introduced Autism Spectrum Disorder. The current understanding of ASD is that it can consist of varying degrees of impaired social development, compromised communication skills, cognitive rigidity in changing sets, and motor differences in comparison to the same areas in neurotypical (NT) children. These differences often severely restrict how autistic children experience development and subsequent mainstream living as it relates to quality of life. Fortunately for autistic children today, the evolution of our knowledge has led to the development of more appropriate assessment tools, earlier intervention programs, and support for families and caregivers. Further, its entry into a mainstream mental and educational dialogue means an even more hopeful future for kids on the spectrum.

The challenges of "fitting in"

Less understood, however, are the interpretations and needs of autistic adults, the majority of whom grew up being labeled as "the weird kid." During their childhood, there were no specialized programs for learning or working outside the mainstream, no attention to the effects of bullying or sexual assault, and no terms such as "special needs." Cultural competency—still a challenge in this enlightened age—was spelled F-I-T I-N. These kids were, and as adults continue to be, required to adapt to their situations, as ever-changing as those were (and are). Furthermore, because there have always been predatory humans seeking to exploit the weak, uninitiated, or different, autistic people (whether diagnosed or not) have been a particularly targeted group. In fact, according to the World Health Organization in 2012, adults with cognitive disabilities had a much higher chance of experiencing a traumatic event (Hughes *et al.* 2012). For reasons explained later, that percentage is likely even higher now. Given that autistic adults commonly experience difficulty in communication, processing those traumas is particularly challenging. Some interventions might even re-traumatize. Thus, supporters could unknowingly contribute to an even greater degree of trauma-related mental health issues. Indeed, having grown up in a time when autism was not a part of the development dialogue, many of these kids have grown into adulthood while experiencing overwhelming situations on a daily basis. And, as adults, they continue to be required to fit in. They are expected to think faster than they might, recognize nuances in conversations, go with the flow, interpret ambiguity, and manage daily, hourly, even by-the-minute overwhelming stimuli, all of which NT people don't think twice about in their own lives.

Autism is a neurological developmental disorder with certain criteria to meet in order to be formally diagnosed. A psychologist diagnosed Lisa in 2010 when she was 47 years old using the *DSM-IV* (APA 2000), a test, talking about life, and her childhood. It was a confirming diagnosis for Lisa although, at first, she continued her lifelong struggle between trying to "fit in" to the NT world and being herself, which often left her feeling conflicted about her diagnosis as if she presented as a problem rather than just being different from a mainstream that works too fast and tends to lose sight of who it's helping. It would be years before she actually accepted her diagnosis.

At times, even with NT autism "experts" who research, write, and treat other autistic people—i.e., people who might know better—Lisa and other autistic people have experienced overwhelming stimulation, such as people talking all at once, bright lights, strong smells, invasion of space, aloneness, and/or confusion regarding social and linguistic nuance, that leave her doubting her chances of fitting in. She and many others on the spectrum tend to feel they are "not enough."

II. Post-traumatic stress disorder
Post-traumatic stress: a history

As for life-threatening and overwhelming experiences, centuries-old literature indicates a long history of likely sufferers of traumatic stress. Indeed, in reading classic authors such as Homer and Dickens, one can find characters suffering from conditions described quite similarly to modern-day PTSD. Both authors tell stories of incredible struggle, loss, frustration, anxiety, depression, deficits of time or memory, and the disappearance of self. Protagonists are betrayed, watch friends die, and wonder why they lived. There is guilt, fear, sadness, and shame. The wars may end, but the battles live on.

More recent history reveals a set of maladaptive symptoms exhibited by First World War soldiers. These were reported by soldiers in sufficient numbers to be diagnosed as specifically related to war. This constellation of symptoms, which was first recognized and then named by the soldiers themselves, was called "Shell Shock." It described physical symptoms such as extreme fatigue, impaired senses, confusion, and nightmares, but with no clear reason for their appearance. Given the numbers of soldiers involved, however, both the British and US Armies embarked upon data collection and subsequent consultation. Though comprised of a number of physical symptoms, Shell Shock was eventually considered to be more psychological than physical, as manifestations of repressed trauma.

Understandably, war creates situations where someone can feel an intense fear for their own life, as well as being forced to act in ways that are contrary to the basic values of life and liberty. The acts required in soldiering and servicing are often at odds with activities of a nurturing household. Also, teamwork being essential to most missions, soldiers on the ground are commanded to do things "for the good of the corps." Looking into the eyes of a dying friend or blowing up a van of subversives only to find it was full of children can easily overwhelm a soldier's sense of self. Right and wrong can be upended. Trying to relate those experiences and such devastating emotions proved difficult to impossible—there were simply no words to describe the aftermath of a crushing trauma. As investigation into war-related stress advanced, our knowledge of trauma also progressed. Eventually, researchers and practitioners were able to transfer that learning to a more generalized population.

Outside of military experiences, students today watch their friends be killed while in an ostensibly safe school environment. Women, men, and others' bodies are sexually assaulted in the "normal" course of a day. Surviving domestic violence is complicated by a lack of support in areas of transportation, housing, and healthcare, as well as by broken justice systems. We are also seeing far more natural and human-made disasters, with recovery time lasting longer and longer. And we as a general population have less and less of the social, educational, and financial help necessary to overcome these challenges. For these and other reasons, anxiety disorders are now affecting up to 34 percent of various adult populations (Bandelow and Michaelis 2015).

Research into trauma

Provided a trauma is severe enough or in multiples, and coping resources scarce enough, the likelihood of developing post-traumatic symptoms is perhaps greater than we know. This is demonstrated in research leading to the development of the Adverse Childhood Experiences (ACEs) assessment. Longitudinal studies in this area have revealed a link between the number of ACEs and lifelong health and social consequences (Felitti *et al.* 1998). For an autistic child, who we know already experiences stress quite differently, it can be assumed that even more areas of life routinely overwhelm coping abilities.

Having assumed that trauma victims were neurotypically wired, research and assessment in the area of trauma has progressed apart from the neurodivergent brain. On the upside, medical and mental health have progressed well in the trauma area, and many NT trauma patients have gone from victim to survivor. However, given that ASD is a neurodivergent condition, what, then, does research proffer regarding the intersection of ASD and PTSD?

III. Co-occurring diagnosis of ASD and PTSD

A moderate review of the literature using various academic databases reveals very little study into the co-occurrence of these diagnoses. Indeed, in his 2015 review of research pertaining to autistic children and trauma, Hoover found very few studies. In the handful he could use, the vast majority used bullying as the potential source of trauma. His review did not include other areas such as child abuse, natural disaster, or indicators of daily sensory overload. In addition to the small number of studies, Hoover surmised that lack of appropriate assessment tools (typically normed on non-autistic subjects), the difficulties inherent in self-reporting for communication-challenged individuals, and the variation of symptomology included on the autism spectrum have made good research difficult to conduct.

Nevertheless, public discourse and subsequent assistance in these areas are greater than ever before. Hopefully, as research with autistic children is better funded and gains ground, more autistic children will be subjected to fewer trauma-provoking situations, more will be supported with greater understanding, and more will grow into adulthood with a greater quality of life.

So, a pressing question is, what of the autistic people who are currently adults? Most of them grew up in a time without diagnoses, special school programs, or knowledgeable caregivers in this area. Before after-school programs there were multitudes of latch-key kids. Many current adults grew up in a time where bullying, sexual assault, and domestic violence weren't recognized, discussed, or treated. All of this is compounded on the knowledge that people on the spectrum have overwhelming experiences in ways a non-autistic person couldn't imagine. With difficulty in expression of knowledge and emotion, it is proffered that autistic people are more prone to chronic traumatization (Angelone 2017; King 2010).

Lisa writes:

> Imagine having a day of confusion, misunderstanding, hurtful comments, sensory overload, and feeling like you don't belong in this world or to anyone in it. Now imagine living that way over and over and over...as your "normal" day.

Finding the right fit

Lisa, and so many others, continually try to adapt to a world in which they are constantly at odds. Even for an autistic person with a Master's degree, a phrase such as "See you later" can cause hours of energy spent trying to figure out things like: "When is later?"; "Will they see me later today?"; "Should I wait around for them?"; "Are they coming to my house?"; "Should I clean?"; "What does 'see' mean?"; "Are we just going to see each other or are we going to talk?"; "What do they want to talk about?"; "Did I do something wrong?"; "We just saw each other"; "It must be me"; "I said or did something wrong."

Meanwhile, MaryD, who was initially unaware that Lisa was on the spectrum, couldn't connect things together into a workable diagnosis. Lisa's apparent resistance to paperwork, rigid thinking, and difficulty processing seemingly insignificant experiences were indicative of any of several diagnoses. In fact, it was several weeks and a time-break later before Lisa was able to tell MaryD that she felt quite unsettled, because MaryD uses her hands a lot when she speaks; Lisa was too distracted by the movement. She often didn't hear what was being said. Also, if MaryD gave her choices, Lisa would assume that she wasn't working "right" enough or that MaryD didn't want to work with her anymore. Sometimes, Lisa needed to take care of herself in a certain way, but she couldn't communicate that. Memories of rejection, embarrassment, and neglect ran through Lisa's mind— for days (or months).

Both client and provider thought Lisa sought grief therapy as a means of processing her husband's suicide. As often happens, the presenting problem wasn't the only one—it wasn't compartmentalized to death. Though Lisa didn't recognize it at the time, her long-term marriage had been highly abusive, as were parts of her childhood. She had tried therapy before and in some cases felt situational relief. In other cases, she felt even more traumatized—judged for being rude, harsh, or even threatening. Some professionals gave what she interpreted as commands; some she interpreted to have expectations far above what she felt capable of doing. Others treated her as if she were incompetent. One shared their own problems as if Lisa was the therapist. All the while, as she strived to adapt, she felt defective and insufficient, like a substandard human being.

She knew she was autistic, but she didn't connect it to the difficulties in her daily life. Lisa states: "All I wanted was help to understand, but I kept doing it all wrong."

It was clear early on that Lisa had trouble accessing and/or managing her feelings. It was also clear that MaryD wasn't able to use her skills to reach into Lisa's world. It didn't look like a good match.

In searching for referrals, it became clear that—at least regionally—finding practitioners who combined ASD and PTSD was not possible. A subsequent investigation into available resources for adults, both community and academically oriented, was equally disappointing. Thus, both client and practitioner struck a deal: they would work together as equals, both teaching and learning as they moved together towards mutual understanding and treating Lisa's co-occurring symptomology.

Chapter II

Autism Spectrum Disorder in Real Life

What is autism?

Clinicians have some analytical tools at the ready to help with multiple considerations of diagnoses. One of these is the *DSM-V* (APA 2013). The manual is the culmination of decades of work by multitudes of professionals with the intention of streamlining the sometimes-complicated process of diagnosis. The DSM has three sections: diagnostic criteria, diagnostic classification sets, and the descriptive text. The diagnostic criteria lists all the mental health disorders in the DSM, with a standardized code associated with each disorder. The diagnostic classification sets are symptoms and criteria that need to be met to diagnose someone with a disorder. The descriptive text has different sets of information to describe each disorder more specifically. While the DSM is the standard manual used in diagnosing mental disorders, it is only the best we have so far. As research and knowledge have expanded, many diagnoses have undergone significant changes, from newly appearing to further defined, or being deleted as illnesses altogether.

I. Diagnostic criteria

Currently, according to the *DSM-V* (APA 2013), autism spectrum disorder is characterized according to a constellation of symptoms, as follows:

- **Social communication:** The *DSM-V* (APA 2013) states there must be persistent and pervasive deficits in this area marked by problems in social-emotional reciprocity. This means that people with ASD may have an "abnormal social approach and failure of normal back-and-forth conversation." They may not initiate or participate in social interactions or "share in interests, emotions, or affect." They may lack physical aspects of communication such as eye contact and use of body gestures or facial expressions. There may also be problems in recognizing, developing, or maintaining relationships, interest in social interactions, ability to engage in imaginative play, and/or difficulties adjusting their behavior to various social situations.

- **Restrictive, repetitive patterns of behavior, interests, or activities:** This may be manifested via stereotyped or repetitive motor movements or use of language (e.g., echolalia, lining up objects, idiosyncratic phrases). There may be an inflexible adherence to routines, difficulty with change—even seemingly very small changes—rigid thinking patterns, and an inability to smoothly change sets. Intense interest or fixation on objects or events and extreme sensitivity or unusual disinterest in the sensory environment, such as regarding pain, temperature, food, textures, light, sound, or smell are also common.

- **Symptoms:** These are present from early development, although they might not be formally diagnosed until much later due to reasons such as the degree of social support or coping skills. It is also important to remember that autism was not well known when many current adults were children. Also, autistic women do not present in the same manner as autistic males, which hinders the diagnostic process for them. Jolynn Haney found, "Despite limited research, there is evidence that criteria used to identify autism are gender-biased, leaving females with autism undiagnosed or misdiagnosed" (Haney 2016). Autistic women are overlooked and many times misdiagnosed with borderline personality disorder (BPD), bipolar disorder, or attention deficit hyperactivity disorder (ADHD) (Muller, 2019). Autistic women tend to be more socially able, although it costs them a lot due to masking (Bargiela, Steward and Mandy 2016).

- **Impairment:** This must significantly impact daily functioning across a broad area of functioning.

In addition to the above and the varying number of specific criteria that must be met for consideration of an ASD finding, assessment also needs to be sensitive to varying degrees of an issue. Also, co-occurring disorders such as intellectual disability or language impairment, associated medical or genetic factors, or neurodevelopmental features need consideration. Add in the possibility of differential diagnoses, and that's a fair amount of information to which non-specialized practitioners or first responders must attend. Objectively, though, it's learnable through formalized resources.

Autism is one of the ever-more clearly refined disorders. Research expanded over the past 20 years has revealed that, rather than being a single condition, autism occurs on a spectrum. Spectrum disorders, put simply, encompass a wide range of symptoms that are connected in some ways but can present in a myriad of ways. It is a complicated condition and, since it is a developmental disorder, there is no "cure." Still, knowledge and cooperation can go a long way to improving the quality of life for many autistic individuals. But life is lived subjectively. What do all of these categories and considerations really mean in the everyday life of an ASD adult?

II. Neurological makeup
The brain and ASD

The human brain is an extraordinarily complex structure. It only weighs about three pounds on average but has tens of thousands of miles of blood vessels and billions of synapses passing messages all around; it never turns off. While each brain is as unique as a fingerprint, there are some features that show up consistently. Some current information about the ASD brain is as follows:

One characteristic that appears nearly universal when discussing the functioning in autistic adults is that of heterogeneity. The autistic brain, while consistent under the umbrella areas of difficulty with social skills, communication, and unusually narrow areas of interest, is as cognitively and behaviorally diverse as any other human brain type. Some people on the spectrum are considerably less verbal than others; some can claim success in the working world whereas others struggle in a work environment; some can "mask it" in social settings for longer periods of time than others, or not at all. Some learn to trust, whereas others don't; still others have varying degrees of that trust in certain circumstances on certain subjects—always with the chance of having it come crashing down on them. All of these things can be going on at once, and helpers might never know the difference.

How, then, might the ASD brain be so different from an NT brain? As with so many other areas of autism, research is limited but the questions are vast. The perpetual arguments in the nature–nurture debate provide many directions of study.

One such trend is towards parts of the brain that interpret body language.

Research in this area has found a variance in the temporal lobe, where visual input connects (Cheng *et al.* 2015). Things in the temporal lobe work differently for an autistic person versus an NT person. For example, appropriate social behaviors in the NT population are largely reinforced by interpreting facial expressions. From early development, children learn to distinguish facial expressions and subsequent meanings by mirroring the caretaker and repeating behaviors that produce positive reinforcement. They monitor responses and learn who to go near and who to avoid, or when to smile and how to get the cookie. Thus develops the NT ability to evaluate and adjust as a means to an end, for example, of pleasing a friend on her birthday, acting appropriately at church, or working on a team.

With time, the nuances of life situations are learned and known almost naturally. The NT child, for example, typically learns to cooperate with someone in one situation but seeks added support in another. They may know that they have to approach a certain person even if they don't want to, but not another. They learn social responses may be different from family ones. Over time, they can reasonably predict cause and effect. They learn about others and themselves. For autistic children, these kinds of cognitions are challenging, because their brain operates differently. Due to differences in the temporal lobe, autistic people have skills related to memory, sensory information, and emotions that operate outside of the typical NT abilities. Nuances NTs take for granted tend to be mysterious to most autistic people.

A related direction in identifying brain differences may be in how the brain integrates and connects information. For example, in brain imaging of NT and ASD adults, Just *et al.* (2004) found that NT brains have a "rhythmic synchronicity" whereby different parts of the brain work together smoothly in the integration and recall of information. In emotional feeling, for example, the front parts work with parts nearer the back to correctly interpret and coordinate input. In a brain with autism, however, there appears to be less synchrony between brain parts, that is, some areas appear to work independently of others. The authors posit this as a major reason for the difficulty in autistic people to attend to faces, read their expressions, and/or recognize emotions. Without that ability, mirroring, repeating, and interpreting are as confusing as an unlearned foreign language in a strange culture. This discovery might also explain deficits in working memory and sequence learning. Also, the spatial functions typically mediated by the parietal lobe might be complicated by the lack of synchronized functioning.

What does it feel like to be autistic?

Lisa shares:

> Being autistic is a lot like feeling alone. For most of my life, I have not fit in with my peers. In grade school, I was bullied, rejected, and ignored by my peers. In college, I had friends, but not the social competency to keep myself safe or to make any meaningful friendships. In the workplace, my work ethic of focusing on my work and not socializing was taken advantage of by my bosses giving me an unfair amount of work just because I could complete it. As a mother, meeting the social needs of my children required me to be in many social situations, and the same type of "not fitting in" I experienced in grade school happened on an adult level.
>
> It's a world of thinking in pictures. I can see the answers to problems in my mind, sometimes in 3D and sometimes on a whiteboard in my mind. My memories are movies that play in my head of what happened. When I experience a memory, I can see everything in detail. I see the environment such as it was when the actual event happened.

I have intense passions. I love information, from intellectual lectures, any kind of documentary, podcasts, current events, and reading non-fiction genres. I have an insatiable curiosity for all things in nature, science, and weird unexplainable phenomena. I love sharing ideas and interesting facts with others as much as I love others sharing them with me.

Colors mean more than just the perception of the reflection of wavelengths of visible light. Colors can be comforting, neutral, or distressing to me. Purple is the color I connect with the most. Purple is a very comforting, calming color for me. I have colors that are neutral to me, as well as colors that cause unpleasant feelings of unease, depression, and impending doom.

I'm different than the people in my life. It's a feeling I grew up with and still have today. I've always known I was different, but I didn't know why until I was diagnosed at 47 years old, although I suspected it for years. The differences are not superficial. The differences are neurological. They are not wrong per se, just different, yet different enough to cause disruptions in many areas of my life such as connecting with people, bullying, and not fitting in with my peers or society in general.

It feels like I missed out on the hidden curriculum of life, where other people just seem to know how to connect, make friends, and sustain relationships. Instead, I need to put an enormous amount of effort into meeting people, starting conversations, and keeping relationships moving forward. Still, many times I'm alone, unable to get beyond the confusion, emotional exhaustion, and disappointment when yet another friendship fails and I don't know why.

It feels like never being understood. It feels like trying to do the right thing all the time, just to find out I've failed and made wrong decisions socially. Social interactions can feel like walking through a minefield where the mines are analogous to social blunders and no matter how hard I try to get around them or to diffuse them, they blow up anyway.

It feels like I wake up in a world where the environment was not made for me. The lights are too bright, noises hurt my ears, clothing is uncomfortable, smells can be extremely unpleasant, and people all speak a different language, such as body language and social nuances. My senses are assaulted continually throughout the day. I can't walk down the cleaning aisle in a grocery store where there are shelves of laundry detergent, cleaning supplies, and scented candles without feeling like I can't breathe and becoming overwhelmed by all the smells. Loud noises physically hurt my ears, and to me loud noises can be an announcement in a store, a radio, someone yelling, brakes squealing, a baby crying, a horn honking, someone whistling, and many more.

I'm a literal thinker in a figurative world, which at times can be as frustrating as it can be hilarious. The frustration comes when other people don't mean what they say or say what they mean and I have no idea what is actually being said to me, and I seldom have time to figure it out. The hilarity comes when I take phrases literally, such as "Go jump in a lake," "He has a chip on his shoulder," or "I'm in a pickle."

Autism has given me my creativity, which includes the skill to write, the enjoyment of details, an insatiable curiosity, a thinking mind, the ability to see outside the quadrilateral, honesty, fairness, and a connection to colors that I know are different than in other people. These qualities are what offset the difficulties so I can try to reach a balance someday and be at peace with being autistic.

As is indicated by the above, people with ASD generally feel apart from the world. The mainstream population is such because the majority of NTs have brains that work similarly to each other. With ASD, however, the brain works differently...which makes all the difference.

Memory

An area of memory that Lisa and many others struggle with is autobiographical memory. This type of memory consists of two categories—semantic and episodic—which aid in three areas that help people to connect socially. Those areas are directive, self, and social (Vranić, Jelić and Tonković 2018). Semantic memory stores facts and hard data whereas episodic memory consists of experiences, stories, and past perceptions. NT people use both parts in everyday activity, even for the most basic interactions. When a person approaches them, they'll search their memory to figure out if they have ever met before, what was discussed and/or experienced, and their perception of the person (dangerous? friendly? pleasant? wary?). They'll appraise the other, perhaps by looking at clothing or other items for hints of commonality or conversation topics. They might also try to pull up memories of other people or events that could relate, or any other things that could be used as a short- or long-term bonding exercise.

With autistic brains, however, it appears that there is a disconnection in autobiographical memory (Just *et al.* 2004). Lisa notes that while she has a strong memory for facts she finds interesting, she has trouble remembering emotional experiences. For example, Lisa reports that when she's involved in a conversation, she spends a lot of time trying to determine if what she's seeing or feeling is "correct." She's unsure of what social cues she's missed and tries to figure this out, too, before responding. She notes, "sometimes I realize I didn't listen... because I'm trying to decide what to say next, or how to interpret what someone is saying." This interrupts the necessary flow of information into short-, then long-term memory. Thus, she tends to miss the gist of many conversations.

Communication

Memory is also involved in even more basic parts of performing in social interactions. Though non-autistic people usually don't realize it, when they talk to someone else, they are listening, registering information and its meaning, and using stored semantic and episodic memories while formulating responses at lightning speed (DeWeerdt 2016); so quick, in fact, that everything goes together seamlessly. For an autistic person, however, things are likely very different. Due to the divergence in memory and connectivity, autistic people often get behind in a conversation. For Lisa, her memories aren't complete and don't come fast enough. She doesn't always know what someone is talking about and before she can ask a question, the topic expands or changes and confusion compounds. Combined with lighting, din, activity in the room, and other sensory challenges, it's often necessary for her to withdraw. Lisa states, "Still, even after I withdraw, it always feels like there is an unresolved issue between me and the other person that needs to be worked out before proceeding further in developing the relationship." In fact, many autistic people tend to perseverate on a conversation that they perceive went wrong until they can figure out what happened, which can take a long time because they decipher it word by word, extensively. However, the other person may not have experienced any dissonance at all.

Social communication

The *DSM-V* (APA 2013) states there must be persistent and pervasive deficits in this area, marked by problems in social-emotional reciprocity. This means that ASD people may be perceived as acting weird or focusing "wrong" as compared to the mainstream. For example, they may not initiate or participate in social interactions or connect with others' interests or feelings. They may lack physical aspects of communication such as eye contact and use of body gestures or facial expressions. There may also be problems in recognizing, developing, or maintaining relationships, interest in social interactions, ability to engage in imaginative play, and/or difficulties adjusting their behavior to various social situations. Much of this is true for Lisa. She writes:

> My first memory of difficulty with social communication was in first grade. I was at the playground, and a girl named Jill approached me with a few other girls and asked me some questions. She asked why I acted the way I did, why I was so quiet, and basically—why was I so weird. I can remember wanting to know those answers too, but I had no idea. The result of her questioning was her validation that I was different, and the beginning of the way my peers treated me up until I graduated from high school 12 years later. They bullied, teased, rejected, ostracized, and just left me out of their lives. I pretty much spent my social life watching from the sidelines if I was lucky; and if not lucky, I got a negative, fully exposed social experience. Those were my two default states—invisible or bullied.
>
> I never got the chance to develop skills around social-emotional reciprocity during my developmental years. I didn't have regular conversations with my peers. The conversations I had with my teachers were one-sided, with the teachers leading the conversations around schoolwork. It never crossed my mind to advocate for myself. I never thought I had any control over what happened in my life.
>
> As far as initiating or participating in social interactions, on the rare occasions when I took a chance and did try,

it never ended well, so I kept to myself most of the time. I had no friendships to make, develop, and maintain during my younger years. I had no interest in games of imaginative play, so most of what I did in my free time was ride my bike, read, and just be outside by myself. Even apart from brain structure, it's hard to figure out how to do something if you never get the chance to practice or be allowed to make mistakes.

As I grew up, the way I gained any social skills was by watching thousands of different social interactions, sitting on the sidelines over many years. I took what I liked and left the rest. I read books on etiquette and paid attention to how characters in books and movies socially interacted with each other. I had no real practice with those social skills I'd learned about though, because most of the time I was alone. Still, I learned how to mask my lack of social skills to fit in the best I could.

As I have lived through grade school, college, singlehood, marriage, motherhood, and now being a widow, I have had to grow and change those social skills as I learn along the way what is best. I have social skills for different social situations and seem to be liked by people in general. It's exhausting. I'm always checking myself. It's a lot of work to know what to say, when to say it, where to look, the right distance to stand away, how long to talk, how to begin a conversation, how to end a conversation, and to figure out what is really being said, which everyone else except for me seems to understand. Yet I do all of these things even though it's hard and I don't want to do them, because I want to have connections with people. I manage by masking. I mask my autism to fit in, and even though I'm still alone behind my mask, at least I am able to socialize a bit. Although masking costs a lot in energy and confusion, I don't know how else I can get my needs met.

What I've found over the years is that social communication is variable depending on many factors such as who I'm talking to, how many people I'm talking to, whether it's business or personal, and the environment. It is variable to the point where there are no patterns to follow, the rules are changed from one person to the next, and it's impossible to "be ready" for the infinite number of possibilities of social interactions.

I find it helps to use logic with *if/then* statements to socialize. For example, *if* a person you know walks right by you without interacting, *then* they either didn't see you or they are preoccupied. *If* you purposefully say hello to them, *then* they say hello to you amiably, everything is ok. *If* you purposefully say hello to them, *then* they walk away as if they didn't hear you, there is something wrong. There are thousands of *if/then* statements to be used in all kinds of social interactions, which is one reason why it can be so exhausting to socialize.

Emotions

Communication is not always about words. Indeed, often autistic (and other) people can't find the words to identify feelings. For Lisa, colors have always been important in terms of emotions. She may not be able to identify the appropriate feelings or verbalize certain thoughts, but she can give them colors, which gives her hints on what might be coming next. Her body, too, will tell her things she couldn't express, though it took her a while to figure that out. She shares:

I'm not great at knowing what emotion I'm feeling most of the time. I know I'm upset when I get a stomachache. For years I would tell my husband, children, and relatives that I had a stomachache if I wanted them to understand I was feeling badly, but that was all I could explain. I had no emotions I could attach to my stomachache. If my stomachache got too bad, I would know it was time to leave a place or have some time alone. I can remember having a lot of stomachaches as a child, too. I was taken to the doctor to find out the reason why. Finally, the doctor told my mother there was nothing wrong with me and to just let me go out and play. I remember that day. I remember feeling misunderstood by everyone involved, knowing my stomachaches were not just in my head, and trying to decide who to trust—myself or the doctor. I never complained about my stomachaches as a child again, so I'm pretty sure I didn't choose to trust myself. I accepted stomachaches as a part of my life being a barometer of my emotions.

As an adult, Lisa still feels her emotions in her body. She reports having:

a shaky feeling inside my torso, and a pain in my neck, chest, and/or stomach. A feeling of panic can be felt as a pain in my chest, a huge lump in my throat, constriction of my windpipe, a headache, and/or the feeling of impending doom.

As such, her body can tell her that she's having feelings. She may not be able to identify her feelings or make a plan to manage them, and they can completely debilitate her. The more intense the body feelings are—up to the point of whole-body pain—the stronger those feelings are. Her feelings are communicating to her, but she can't communicate them to herself or anyone else.

Repetition and routine

Because an autistic person already has so much stimulation to attend to, being able to count on some form of routine is pretty important. It may seem like just a TV program, a seat in the same place every day, all the pencils in order, or being picked up in the blue car, but it isn't. Routine and repetition are forms of safety. It precludes the need for guessing or imagining, which tends to use more energy from an already horribly short supply.

Lisa goes on to explain:

I like routine. I need routine. I count on routine. Change is too difficult. Change is unnerving. Change is too volatile. For example, when I leave my house to go somewhere, I have already thought about what is going to happen many times over before I leave. I've thought about who is going with me, how far I have to drive, what the weather is like, who is going to be there, how long I will be gone, what we'll be doing, how long I will have to stay, what I'm going to say when I want to leave, conversation starters I might need, who I may need to stay away from, what coping skills I may have to use, and the many more social requirements I have to meet before I come back home again. I think about all of this to feel safe, confident, and secure in being able to go where I'm going. If there is a change to any of that, all of the preparation I've gone through feels meaningless, and it leaves me with no preparation about what's going to happen next, which causes high anxiety almost immediately. Anything can happen and I'm not ready at all. I must be prepared ahead of time in order to be successful socially. I can't successfully wing it, which is what I'm forced to do when there is a change. Typically, what happens is I have high anxiety, suddenly find myself fighting off panic, can't think at all, and am at the mercy of the people I'm with, the environment I'm in, and my anxiety. I withdraw for safety, possibly go into an automatic pilot mode, and head for home as quickly as possible.

My thoughts, on a minute-by-minute basis:

And the advantages

It's important to know, however, that not everything is negative about being autistic. In fact, there are also some pretty wonderful parts about it.

Lisa shares:

Many times, when I engage in *problem-solving*, I can see the answer in my thoughts; whether it is solving a mechanical/ engineering problem or a business problem, the solutions come to me in pictures. Once I was in a staff meeting discussing a schedule that included times for us to have a lunch break. At first glance it seemed impossible to have enough coverage while each of us took turns having a break. I got quiet and thought about all the different combinations of a schedule until I "saw" one that would work. I told my colleagues it could be done and I'd have the schedule written down as soon as possible. They were skeptical, but agreed. Sure enough, the schedule was made and we all started having lunch breaks.

Another useful part of having autism is *heightened senses*. I'm going to be honest and say most of the time dealing with my senses is a negative experience, but there have been several times where I smelled something burning before anyone else did and was able to stop a potentially dangerous situation before it got too bad. Once, I was at work and could smell something off. It was faint at first, and I was the only one who could smell it. The next day I still was the only one who could smell it and I still didn't know what it was exactly. The third day, the smell was so potent I got a headache and my sinuses hurt. I started walking around the building to try to find out what was causing the smell. One of my colleagues finally smelled it too, although very faintly and couldn't place it either. I went upstairs to check a couple of rooms that were never used, and there was a door leading to the roof. I couldn't stand to be up there more than a few seconds, the smell was so strong. It was gas fumes. Someone power washing the roof had left an industrial-sized power washer in the room next to the door to the roof. The whole room was full of gas fumes, a very dangerous situation.

I also have a *love of words* that I attribute to autism. A high vocabulary is a common aspect of autism, specifically for those diagnosed with Asperger's Syndrome, which was my original diagnosis. I enjoy the way some words sound, love definitions of words, the spelling of words, and relish finding the exact word to fit in a sentence to communicate precisely what I want to say. I love putting words together to make stories, write my thoughts, and communicate.

Another gift of autism is *empathy*. I have such deep empathy for people; I can feel their pain and some other emotions I can't name but can definitely feel. Although my relationships with people have been confusing, bullying, and hurtful throughout the years, I still have strong compassion and empathy for people, especially those going through a painful time in their lives. There is a prevalent misconception that autistic people lack empathy; in reality, most of them have so much empathy it hurts. Also, autistic people tend to mask their true selves, so any empathy they might be feeling would be masked as well.

I believe the *creativity* I have is another positive aspect of autism. It's part of being different. Creativity is a different way of looking at life and the world. It's looking outside the box, taking risks, and having confidence in unconventional ideas. Creativity can show through art, music, writing, baking, problem-solving, and any other hobby, passion, or endeavor.

Thus, in looking at some of the negative and positive aspects of ASD, it becomes clear that ASD is a different way of thinking, and in many ways quite valuable to society in general. The struggle is not about autistic individuals fitting in; it's about how non-autistic people can accept what a neuro-divergent person can offer. Indeed, most people on the spectrum are less interested in being pitied than they are in being understood and helped to understand. They want presumed competence. They want to work together with NTs and all neurodiverse people in order to live an enriched life.

Lisa writes:

Autistic adults diagnosed later in life are advocating for themselves and others, gaining life skills, fulfilling lifelong dreams, and meeting their goals while battling things like social communication problems, sensory difficulties, interpersonal relationship problems, and intrapersonal conflict, with little to no understanding or support. Knowing first-hand of the personal struggles and constant striving it takes to reach those goals, I admire autistic people for their resilience, perseverance, and courage. What we want and what is needed is not awareness as much as it is acceptance of who we are as a people group.

III. Inherent vulnerabilities

Autistic adults are at a disadvantage due to characteristics inherent to autism. Social nuances often render them vulnerable to being naive in situations where it would help to be socially savvy and aware that harm is coming their way. Social skills are also important in all areas where adults want to be successful, such as being hired for employment, being successful in school, experiencing meaningful relationships, healthcare, and many other social situations. Difficulties with social interactions in these key areas leave autistic people in vulnerable situations where they could be bullied, taken advantage of, abused, and/or misunderstood to the point where they might be fired, fail in school, have poor healthcare, and/or experience tumultuous relationships.

Sensory difficulties

Lisa shares:

I am not fully at peace with my environment, inside or out.
Outside, I can relax and enjoy nature for the most part, especially the ocean and mountains of New England. I love a campfire with the crackling sounds, warmth, and soft, flickering

light, the sound of a babbling brook, the crunch of snow, bird song, ocean waves, and many other elements of nature. That said, raindrops on my face, neck or arms are very painful. I feel them as sharp needles. Screeches from birds of prey hurt my ears. Some smells are too intense and it's hard to take a breath; or I taste what I smell, which is very unpleasant.

Inside, sounds can be irrepressible to the point where the only solution is to leave. Sounds are torturous sometimes. Some examples are: if a person constantly taps their pencil; if someone shouts; a dripping sound; alarms going off are excruciating; and the din of many people talking all at once is difficult as well. I can't hear a person I'm right next to if there's any background noise. In an auditorium it's even more difficult to hear a speaker if someone near me is rustling paper, whispering, shuffling their feet, coughing, or making any kind of noise. When I'm in a restaurant or lunchroom where there are many conversations going on at once, I hear a little bit from each one around me and I can't participate in any at all.

Colors can help me feel safe and peaceful, or cause me to become uneasy and uncomfortable. I'm color sensitive and colors have a direct effect on my emotions. Colors can be the reason I stay in or go from a place, they help change my mood from low to high or vice versa, or they change my health to having or not having a headache/stomachache.

I can remember the first time I used purple. I'm not sure how old I was, except that I was very, very young. I was coloring at a table in the playroom of the lime-green house I grew up in. I pulled orange out of the crayon box first and thought it was pretty. Next, I pulled out purple and immediately felt calm and peaceful. I was mesmerized by the color purple. The connection I made with purple in that moment has lasted my whole life.

Touch is a sensory difficulty which I'm always on the lookout for when arriving or leaving a social situation.

Hugs are nice if I'm aware they are coming, I know and trust the person I'm hugging, and they don't last too long. It sounds picky, but there are reasons for those boundaries. From my experience, a person who impulsively hugs comes in fast and hard. If I'm unaware, the hug can feel more like a tackle. Hugs from people I don't know or trust feel like a violation of my personal space and also extremely uncomfortable. A hug has a time limit. I don't usually have to talk about this—if it's a bit long for me, pulling away a bit usually does the trick. I have had hugs that go on for too long and I feel trapped. If someone doesn't understand the touch sensitivity or is unsure of what to do, I'd rather not have a hug. Mostly, I'd just like to be asked, and if I need a hug, I ask for one.

Social skills deficits

Lisa shares:

Social anxiety causes difficulty in starting conversations, ending conversations, handling one-sided conversations, understanding when someone is uninterested, knowing when it's time to talk, getting behind in the conversation, and then trying to catch up. Not understanding people because they don't say what they mean or mean what they say hinders my attempts in following and understanding conversations.

Theory of mind refers to the ability for one to understand that thoughts, feelings, perceptions, and knowledge are different for oneself and everyone else. While it is typically developed in childhood, people on the spectrum are sometimes challenged in this area. Perhaps it is because these things are theoretical rather than concrete, or because theory of mind requires one to hold lots of different perspectives in mind while engaging in social or professional activities. This is likely one of the reasons that many ASD people focus on actions.

As Lisa states:

> The only way to tell something about someone is by their actions. There's no way to tell anything about a person by their intentions: "The road to Hell is paved with good intentions." Actions, outcomes, and results are the only indicators anyone can look at to know what kind of a person someone is; and with me, there's even one more step: it's what they do with the outcome. If there's a good reason for a different outcome than they said would happen, I'd understand because, in life, mistakes and circumstances happen to everyone, but it would take me a lot of thinking and complicated feelings to get to that understanding. Open and honest communication about why a different outcome happened would be very helpful in understanding.

Processing speed is also a characteristic of autism that has been shown to hinder social skills in adults (Haigh *et al.* 2018).

Lisa shares:

> Processing speed is negatively correlated to anxiety, something that most autistic adults live with day by day. Intelligence is not indicated by processing speed. One trouble with a slow processing speed is not being able to keep up with conversations, especially when there are multiple people having a discussion. Whether it's a business meeting, social gathering, or colleagues brainstorming a solution, processing speed gets in the way of being able to participate in those discussions successfully. What I have done to try to offset my slow processing speed is to think ahead. I can, at times, see where the conversation is going, think ahead to any possible solutions that may work, so when the conversation reaches

where I've gone ahead, I can participate and essentially hide my slow processing speed. This works mostly in staff meetings, business meetings, or working with colleagues. It doesn't work at all with social conversations because there's really no way to predict where the conversation is going. In those instances, I will either follow one person and be able to participate along with that person's thought process only, or I will be very quiet and be a listener. I have yet to be able to participate in a conversation with more than two people successfully unless it's with my kids, people I know well, or the conversation is being facilitated by a group leader.

Misunderstandings

Typical misunderstandings are usually the result of autistic people being literal and neurotypical people using the subtle nuances of speech. For example, to Lisa "Let's get a cup of coffee sometime," means someone has asked her to join them at a coffee place at some unspecified time to get an actual cup of coffee to drink while they talk, hopefully about something substantive and not small talk.

She states:

Although I have learned that "Let's get a cup of coffee sometime" to a non-autistic person many times means a greeting with no actual plans to get coffee, this type of misunderstanding leads to hurt feelings because I feel lied to and can't logically come up with what they said meaning anything different from what the words actually mean. I also feel cheated out of having a cup of coffee with the person, which may have been the only invitation to socialize I got in a while. It's disappointing. The person may not understand why I'm upset at all because to them, all they said was "Hello." I believe what happens is, over time the neurotypical person gets tired of the miscommunication, the friendship is too much work to clarify and communicate and they just stop interacting, taking phone calls, texts, and any other form of contact. I don't understand the lack of contact, blame myself for having done something wrong that I have no idea at all what it could have been, and I start believing I don't belong in this world. I don't fit in and it's all my fault.

Miscommunications

Miscommunication is even more problematic than a misunderstanding. The difference is that miscommunication is more often due to unclear messages between two or more people, such as what can happen between cultures.

Lisa states:

I spent two months visiting both Germany and Denmark, a month visiting China and grew up living in the USA. Although I'm more comfortable in the USA, I still have some of the same problems here communicating as I did in the countries I visited. As I tried to communicate at stores, restaurants, hotels, and tourist areas in the countries I visited, there were many miscommunications due to language and the local culture I violated inadvertently. As I try to communicate here in my own country while speaking my native tongue, I still have miscommunications with other people due to language and cultural differences. One difference in language is autistic people in general are literal. They say what they mean and mean what they say. NTs have nuanced communication that is confusing to autistic people. One example is that when I hear a neurotypical person say they are "in a pickle," I picture them actually in a pickle, or if they say they are going to "run to the store" and then get into a car and drive, I figure they just changed their minds. Although I know what most of the idioms really mean, it's hard to trust when there are such inconsistencies in what is said, and it's difficult to know what to say back in a conversation because many times the people don't mean what they say.

Cultural differences include different ways of socializing. While some autistic people do enjoy a lot of people, concerts, dancing, amusement parks, and so on (yet still may need a quiet place to recharge and regulate), many autistic people prefer a small group of people in a quiet place, talking about meaningful subjects. Small talk is frustrating for many because most of the time it's an exercise in reiterating the obvious, or it's about arbitrary subjects only interesting to the person talking, for example: a sale on shoes, an unknown great aunt's new puppy, or the weather.

It is also mysterious because no one participates in small talk the same way. There are people who pour out their life story as soon as you meet them, some people are very formal and give information about themselves that reveals very little, or sometimes there's the "danger" of a hug like you've just been reunited with a best friend—only it's really a stranger. Small talk can be very frustrating to autistic people.

On the other hand, small talk for non-autistic people has many useful possibilities. Sociologists tend to view small talk as far more important than the term implies. In general, it is usually a way of bonding in a particular situation. Non-autistic people use small talk to share parts of themselves and to try and find commonalities with another, often in a low-risk environment. It can be used to inform the listener about the speaker, or vice versa. It can convey warmth or affection; it can also develop respect or trust. People who use small talk effectively can learn things about others and consider different perspectives. It can put people at ease and comfortable enough to let another into their life space. One might invite another to a book group, or sports tryout, or even a job interview. Strangers meet, engage in small talk, and "go from there."

Reviewing the above, it is understandable that autistic people have difficulty recognizing the benefit of small talk. As it's often used to develop an emotional or social connection that can lead to other possibilities, it is often a mystery to autistic people who enjoy having conversations about things that interest them...which is not usually the weather. Thus, because it's such an accepted and often integral part of socializing in the NT world, an autistic person is more likely to experience isolation in mainstream social settings, missing out on connecting in-the-moment as well as in the kinds of relationships that come from employing small talk. For an autistic person, small talk is "something to get through" because it's common, just not understandable. Rather, autistic people prefer communicating on-line or in small gatherings as they tend to communicate directly and efficiently.

IV. Isolation

Isolation has been a part of Lisa's life for as long as she can remember. For her, the feeling of isolation is a mixture of aloneness and rejection, and being unwanted, invisible, unworthy, scared, lonely, and sad. The mixture of all those feelings together day after day can cause an autistic adult to feel like they do not belong in this world and maybe even want to leave it.

Lisa writes:

I can only imagine what it feels like to be accepted among my offline peers. I've tried to grasp what that might feel like my whole life. The shunning by society in general leaves a person with pervasive aloneness that is difficult to live with long term.

In fact, isolation is unhealthy in that it can lead to an impaired immune system, and an increase in inflammation in the body, which can then lead to premature death due to Type II diabetes, heart disease, and/or arthritis to name a few resulting conditions: "Studies of elderly people and social isolation concluded that those without adequate social interaction were twice as likely to die prematurely" (Olien 2013).

Many autistic adults diagnosed later in life are isolated due to having grown up without help in learning how to socialize and communicate with people, including Lisa, who shares:

If I have participated in a positive, engaging social interaction that leaves me hopeful I have connected with another person, the act of leaving them when the interaction has ended always brings that connection to a close as if it never happened. The connection may be renewed the next time we are together, but will dissipate once again after the visit is over.

Lisa also explains how confusing it can be to interact with a person over coffee and feel very close to them, yet, after they part, the feeling of connectedness wanes with physical distance until she doesn't have a concept of the relationship.

Lisa shares:

When I'm with a person, I feel connected. When we are apart, over time, I feel disconnected. It's as if we never connected.

To Lisa, this is another ingredient of loneliness: the inability to feel connected in *absentia*. It's a very real and painful concept.

V. Lack of training in real-life situations

While the diagnostic criteria in the *DSM-V* (APA 2013) are clear, they don't explain what life on the spectrum is really like. The difference between how autism is described with words in the diagnostic manual and what it's actually like being autistic is discouraging. For example, many people say they don't like change; in fact, a typical response to a person who says, "I hate change," is "No one likes change." This is a very minimizing response because the intensity with which many autistic people experience change is often in the overwhelming category, not uncomfortable, or inconvenient—*overwhelming*. When an autistic person is trying to communicate extreme difficulty with change, minimizing the response intensifies the feeling of social isolation, like no one could possibly understand. The autistic person then feels inept and frustrated, or dismissed. The good news is that it might only take one person showing a little compassion to lessen the feeling of isolation.

Lisa states:

> I was in a grief group one night, in the same room with the same people as always, when a moderator came in and announced that we had to change rooms and combine with another group. While everyone else got up to leave—with no problem—I burst into tears. It felt overwhelming to go to a new location with people who might not understand my story the way my regular group-mates did, and it's overwhelming to go to a place I haven't prepared for yet. I did not prepare—picturing the room, walking in, where I would sit, who might be there, etc. One member of the group noticed this. She offered to stay behind until I composed myself. She didn't even say, "If Lisa can come." She said, "*When* Lisa is ready." That made all the difference. She waited, I composed and regulated myself, and we went in together to the new situation. I didn't talk, but

I listened and was able to be there. One person noticing—and not overreacting—can make all the difference, not only in that moment, but maybe even for the next several days.

The work of many great educators and clinicians highlights the disparity between research on various mental differences and real-world practice. They state that the very nature of controlled studies—wherein researchers seek to limit the number of variables that can contaminate the results—means that the outcomes are only possibilities that might happen in exactly the same types of controlled situations. Results contribute to a theory about the broader picture being studied. A theory is a structure of ideas we use to explain something. For example, there are various theories about how the universe develops. Each time science discovers something new, it gets plugged into theory, which is either tweaked or explained away. In the helping fields, we're educated in various theories and use them to make educated guesses on how we think things should go. But the outside world dirties things up, and the "art of practice" begins.

Practice is a complicated reality—where all variables subjective to each individual come into play. It changes the concept and requires adjustment of judgment and direction. Put another way, students of various human services sectors might study a theoretical, standardized definition of a disorder or illness and pass an appropriate academic exam. On paper, they know what to look for and then presumably how to work with it based on theory and past experience. A person's individual world, as unique as a fingerprint, changes things. And more consideration is necessary before an appropriate conceptualization of a most likely diagnosis, and resultant treatment, can be made. This is why practitioners are schooled in the art of differential diagnoses.

VI. Differential diagnoses

Many disorders can look similar, but develop in different ways, with nuanced and important differences. Looking at "differential diagnoses" is a practice that helps practitioners to look at symptoms from different angles and with different accompanying symptoms. It leads to more efficient and effective diagnoses and treatments. Unintended weight gain, for example, can mean a variety of different things ranging from a thyroid disorder to major depression. It could be explained by a tumor, pregnancy, medication side effects, or factors in the patient's social ecology. Thus, weight gain itself doesn't lead anywhere definitive, though it could rule out some things. The professional, therefore, needs to know more. In other words, the patient comes in with a broad symptomology and seeks relief. Before the clinician can know specifically from what, there needs to be an assessment of the broad complaint; things are ruled out and other things investigated. This helps whittle down symptoms into columns or categories. With an authentic collaboration between patient and clinician, an accurate picture of background and current functioning lead to a working diagnosis. As meetings and assessment continue, the diagnosis becomes clearer. Treatment plans can then be adjusted as necessary.

Differential diagnosis is part of good training. It requires a breadth of knowledge, careful consideration, and a willing curiosity. With experience, the diagnostic process becomes less complicated (but still necessary). If the clinician or helper assumes everyone understands things the same, such as that a transition is no big deal, then they miss extremely important details necessary for true diagnosis.

MaryD writes:

As a young adult, I was in a profession that required me to learn a different language pretty fast. I was sent to a quick six-week class with eight other people. We spent days learning and repeating. Of note to me was a particular exercise wherein we learned to ask for directions. We were to learn, "Excuse me, where is the market, please?" We practiced: "*¿Disculpe, dónde está el mercado, por favor?*" We practiced each word multiple times, then phrases, then longer phrases: "*¿Disculpe, ¿Disculpe, ¿Disculpe, ¿Disculpe,*" "*Disculpe, dónde está,*" "*Disculpe, dónde está, dónde está está está está,*" "*Disculpe, dónde está...*" over and over and over until we got it right and it was embedded in our brains. Then we practiced the answer in the same way, "It's two blocks up and one block to the left." Then I went to my assigned country, and I attempted to speak. It so happened that I needed to find the market, so I knew what to ask. Yay, me. The tricky part came when the person did *not* respond that the market was two blocks up and one block to the left. I actually had no clue what he said to me. His response was fast, colloquial, and not what I thought I would hear. What a silly thing to expect! But I learned and that lesson, as embarrassing as it might be, has stayed with me...that what I expected to hear and what I did hear, were two different things, and responses are very important to really listen for.

In taking time to understand from the patient's knowledge and perspective, conceptualizations become much more accurate. The openness to, and the art of, differential diagnosis is important to learn because ASD is often misdiagnosed, to the detriment of patients, caregivers, and the community in general.

Thus, given the little that we really know about the brain and how it interacts with an individual's social ecology, there are many things a professional should consider in the diagnostic process of an ASD person (National Collaborating Centre for Women's and Children's Health 2011). For example, one needs to consider neurological or mental health difficulties such as language delays, intellectual disabilities, coordination disorders,

ADHD or other disorders associated with anxiety, attachment, conduct, regression syndromes, abuse in the home, or sensory impairments.

Processing speed

Time is essential with an autistic person because of varying processing times, anxiety, alexithymia, and the other characteristics of autism. An autistic patient who also has PTSD may not only experience higher levels of anxiety, but is also at risk of experiencing a flashback if they are misunderstood or feel like the clinician is in any way hostile. An autistic client needs more time to appropriate, comprehend, and then communicate what's happening inside. This is usually frowned upon in many parts of society—in medical appointments, banking, ordering from a menu, or everyday "regular" conversation. And the individual might not know how to ask for what they need. In addition, the client may be struggling with many different emotions and stressors yet appear calm and to be functioning fine. One of the commonly frustrating terms that many ASD people hear—signaling that the NTs probably don't understand—is the term "high functioning."

VII. High functioning

First, let's consider the term "high functioning."
Lisa says:

> High functioning means I am able to work extremely hard to hide who I really am so that my autism is mildly experienced by other people. So, I get comments like: "You don't look autistic," "You don't act autistic," "You don't seem autistic," or they say, "I'm autistic too," because I've successfully mimicked NT behavior.

What is meant by high functioning is how well an autistic person is able to change their behavior to mimic those around them to "fit in" socially. It's not copying; that would be much easier. It's the autistic person using their own personality and mimicking the people around them in real time while battling internally about things like social anxiety and deficits in social communication. The effort it takes for an autistic person to look and act like the NT people around them is humongous and exhausting. The term "high functioning" feels like society's requirement for the ASD person to mask so they *do not* act like themselves. The more they don't act like themselves, the better they are liked; the better they are accepted by society.

Lisa adds:

> When that happens to me...I take it as evidence that I don't belong. Also, the more people get to know me, the less high functioning I appear to be and the more our relationship breaks down, so there are two messages here:
>
> One, I'm accepted and can fit in, as long as I work really, really hard to *not* be me.
>
> And two, if I do let someone into my life and start forming a friendship, the closer we get, the more they see the real me and the less they like me until the relationship breaks down. The ultimate message is: I disappointed them. I'm *not* wanted. I'm *not* enough. It's *not* ok to be me.

Also, in Lisa's experience with other ASD adults over various platforms such as social media, lecture halls, and autism-specific publications, she has found the term "high functioning" to be distasteful, even offensive.

Many in the autism community feel that "high functioning" has been developed by neurotypical people to explain something ASD adults have great difficulty explaining. It may even feel at times like the term is more like an NT term for

"I don't have to worry about them." In fact, MaryD stopped using the term when an autistic client asked, "Do you use that term to make yourself feel better about what I go through in my brain?" Though it might sound harsh, that question was asked honestly and without judgment. It was just a very informative question.

In addition, the wording is deceptive. For example, in terms of intelligence, because an IQ score on the Weschler Adult Intelligence Scale-IV (*WAIS-IV*, Wechsler 2008) starts in the Low Average range at 80 and can top out at Extremely High scores above 130, IQ scores leave a pretty wide margin for interpreting the degree of functioning. This, of course, only means things about what can be measured on an intelligence scale. It's useful information, for sure, but it doesn't measure the degree of functioning in society. Thus, more assessment tools are needed for a comprehensive evaluation.

The problem in assessing ASD patients is that assessments for things like depression, anxiety, personality disorders, mania, and so on are normed on non-autistic populations. Also, since autism is largely a social and communication issue, assessment scores are likely not accurate because those assessments are based on the ability for neurotypical communication. Third, if one is extremely talented at illustration, music composition, or computer code but flops at paying bills or managing school, what would be that person's level of functioning? Last, and perhaps most important, there are many autistic adults who are "successful" and appear to do well overall but who struggle internally every minute of every day...and nobody knows it. If they can't communicate in the mainstream, how will they find help for medical emergencies or suicidal ideation?

Indeed, in her advocacy work, Lisa endeavors to educate about the term "high functioning." She states that it is a term used to define autistic people who are holding down jobs, having families, writing books, speaking, researching, advocating, teaching, getting advanced degrees, and so on, all of which are possible for many along the spectrum. It is a deceitful term, though, because autistic adults have to overcome invisible yet formidable obstacles in life to reach those milestones. There are so many struggles to persevere through, stigmas to ignore, and coping skills to use on a minute-by-minute, hour-by-hour, or day-to-day basis. Lisa states, "What I look like on the outside is nowhere near accurate about what's going on inside," and once the external achievement is completed, the internal experience doesn't stop. For these people, the criteria for high functioning is arbitrary and off the mark.

With ASD, things are not "easy" no matter how it looks. Consider the following excerpt from an article called "Just how hard can easy be?" (Morgan 2018a):

> The setting is a classroom. The lead role is an autistic student (played by me). The supporting roles are comprised of the teacher, other students, and any aides in the room. The antagonist is the environment. Let's take a moment and look at a school environment through the eyes of an autistic student.
>
> First, let's consider the setting of a typical classroom in an elementary school. The room is bright and colorful with pictures, charts, a calendar, and completed assignments displayed for all to see. Some colors are neutral, some colors are abrasive, and there's enough of my favorite color to be calming for me. There are desks arranged in a familiar pattern. The books are in the right places, lunch boxes stored away for later, projects left out to finish. There are probably 18–22 kids, one teacher, and an aide or two depending on the day.
>
> The desks are arranged in configurations depending on how the teacher designed the room, and are changed several times during the year—a surprise to the students.

Most students who walk in on those Mornings of Change get excited and the regular noise level is much higher.

For me, those mornings are extremely hard because the change is so abrupt. There is no warning. I'm not excited. I take a step into the room, see the chairs have been moved all around, and I stand still by the doorway, not sure it's my classroom. *My anxiety rises.* I don't know where to go; I don't know where to sit. Who will sit near me? Will I know my new seat mate? Will we get along? *My anxiety rises even more.* I panic—where are the colors? *I want to find my calming color.*

My heart palpitates uncomfortably as I tentatively look at the walls to see if there's change there too. Thankfully the colors are still in the right places, so for today my anxiety calms a little because the colors on the walls haven't been moved.

Still standing by the doorway, I start to tune into the sounds of students talking in different speeds, at different decibels, changing topics, with a squeal or two thrown in along with an argument here and there. *It's so hard to think.* I am still trying to regulate from the change in the desk arrangement and can't move to get my stuff yet. I still don't know which desk is mine. How do I find out which desk is mine? *My panic is uncomfortable.* There are at least 22 desk chairs squeaking on the floor, pencils being sharpened, the teacher giving directions, and students finding their new seats. There's too much to look at, so I focus on a spot on the floor, completely overwhelmed.

Minutes later, I'm still standing in the same spot by the doorway. I stand rooted by panic brought on by the change, the noise, and the confusion about where to sit. *I wish I could find words to explain.* My teacher tells me she wants me to move. She wants me to get ready for the day. If I don't soon, she said she will help me move. *What!* Does that mean she's going to touch me? *Panic!* I don't want her to touch me.

The anxiety I've been working hard to control is rising again. My feet are even more firmly rooted by the doorway.

How can I move if I don't know where my desk went? *I need to find my desk.* The room started out cool, but is quickly warming up with all the students moving around. I feel too warm; my anxiety is heating me up too. The teacher has on a perfume that the other students are all saying smells real nice, but hurts my sinuses, a sweaty student walks by who forgot to put on deodorant, and someone let out an SBD but no one will own up to it. The strong smells are all around me. *My head hurts.* I can't get away from them. *High, high, anxiety!* Still, I can't move.

The teacher warns me again to go get ready for the day. *Now I might be in trouble too!* I want to get ready, but don't know where to go yet. The classroom noises are a cacophony in my ears and I can't think. *I need to move.* Why? I have to find my desk. Where is it again? I never found out. *My mind races as fast as my heart.*

My teacher's voice reaches me again out of all the other voices and it's not comforting. It sounds different—angry, I think. She wants me to say something to her. *I have no words. There's too much to think, feel, and figure out.* What do I do? *Think!* Oh! I still haven't moved because I don't know where to go. How does everyone else know where to go? *So confusing!* My teacher asks if I can see the bright tags on the desk with the students' names on them. *There are tags on the desks?*

The teacher's voice is rising and it's hard to know why? Is it me? *I'm trying so hard!* I move towards the desks, anxiety still high, heart still pounding, still too warm, hearing noises all around me, the strong perfume smell makes it hard to breathe, a student bumps into me, the sudden touch makes me forget everything I was doing and I stand very still once more—all my progress gone. *My panic rises again.* My skin crawls uncomfortably. I can still feel where the student bumped into me. I take a deep breath, I try to ignore all the intrusions on my senses, and with resilience I didn't know I had, I continue walking slowly, deliberately around the desks and find a tag with my name on it. *Relief!* My head hurts from the smells; I'm overstimulated, overwhelmed, so I sit down and gently rock back and forth to calm myself.

My teacher walks over to me and says, "See how **easy** that was? Why aren't you excited like the other students! Now sit up straight and stop rocking in your chair."

I just look at her and no words will come out because they are as stuck inside my head as I was stuck by the doorway. *"No, didn't you see how **hard** it was for me?"* I start to rock, forgetting in the moment, I'm not allowed, so I stop. *What **can** help me?*

VIII. Masking

Masking, also called social camouflaging, is a coping mechanism meant to serve the function of fitting in or, at the least, reducing pressure to do so. Indeed, many ASD adults feel compelled to "act right." ASD people often feel as though they live in a world that "wasn't made for me." They struggle moment by moment to act "properly" and fit in. Many talk about feeling forced to act a certain way but that they don't understand the point. For example, while kids play, adults tend to stand around and make small talk. An ASD person would likely find it very difficult to follow pointless conversation and so might drift off, look "spacy," or otherwise not conform to comfort-bearing situations.

Being part of the NT mainstream comes with the danger of assuming that everything works the way an NT thinks it works; that everyone sees things the same way as the mainstream does. This is a theory/practice problem, too. Indeed, when asked if everyone has the same perceptions or needs, helpers, supervisors, teachers, friends, and family would of course respond in the negative. Theoretically, it is so. In practice, however, NTs are often too busy or too oblivious to consciously put the theory into practice, and judgments can be harsh. Thus, ASD adults have learned that masking—pretending to be upbeat, interested, strong, or ordinary, for instance—is often safer in the moment than the feeling of being a spectacle or a bother. But it comes at a price.

Lisa writes:

> I can't remember starting to wear a mask or ever being without one, except for after becoming aware of masking. Now that I know masking is one of the reasons why I have that feeling of emptiness and aloneness, it's more difficult to continue using it, although I do still use masking quite a lot. Masking is like pretending or acting. It's using skills developed by watching and learning. The problem with masking, and the reason it feels so empty and alone, is that no one ever gets to know me; they only know the person I'm acting as at that time.

The results of masking and autistic "high functioning" are similar. They both leave the autistic person feeling like they can't be themselves to be accepted. Masking is typically referred to as what happens in a social setting, including the workplace, when an autistic adult needs to fit in, look, and act like everyone else. Masking also includes the level of ability to be successful in holding down a job, managing a career, being a parent, getting an education, and the everyday tasks of living independently. Because the severity level of ASD—which determines how much support for which the person is eligible—is based on skills in social communication and certain overt behaviors, many who need services but mask well go unrecognized.

As a long-term solution, however, masking tends to have high costs in terms of quality of life. When someone masks, they can forget the true them. They don't trust themselves or others. They often become confused about what's real for them and so can't know how to judge another as genuine. Combined with the ASD brain's difficulty in semantic and episodic memory, this is yet another double whammy. Social bonds are increasingly difficult to make when someone masks, because as one ASD adult put it, "I'd not know how to interact as myself." Thus, ASD people often feel an added loneliness due to intentionally keeping people away for fear of being found out and disappointing.

Finally, masking costs a great deal in terms of energy—emotionally, mentally, and physically. A person must concentrate intensely, scan to see if they're "doing things right," think of an appropriate response, worry that it wasn't appropriate, control reflexive thinking or feeling, decide whether what someone else is saying is true or a figure of speech, and take care of their discomfort. It is the leading cause of exhaustion and autistic burnout. Yet, if they don't use it, they are in danger of being rejected, ridiculed, ignored, or avoided. It's a delicate balance, and the ASD person often doesn't come out ahead.

IX. What a healthy relationship looks like for ASD

Put simply, healthy relationships occur when each party is getting their needs met in the relationship, when the give-and-take is equitable to both. Friends demonstrate a respect for the other's viewpoints. Willingness to communicate without blame or denigration—in search of understanding—is key to a successful friendship. Add honesty to respect and communication, and there is hopefully a supportive recipe for trust. When two people feel a sense of equity, the friendship exists. The varying degrees of the ingredients proffered and taken determine the strength or satisfaction of a long-term relationship.

For someone on the spectrum, friendships are hard, primarily due to the nature of relationships, which is that most ebb and flow over time. For autistic people, there are many complications that NT people often don't see. For example, autistic people tend to think in rigid patterns. Thus, a major piece of healthy relationships for them is *consistency*. The "ebb and flow" of relationships is puzzling, as is when people say they're going to do something (like call on Wednesday) and they don't do it. Unanticipated change often begets confusion and fear. With autism, the person could interpret sudden silence as if they did something wrong or misinterpreted cues. It's hard for an autistic person to know if a behavior is considered inappropriate, because in an NT world, sometimes it is and other times it isn't. Knowing what to expect is important for autistic people. The fluidity of friend, romantic, and work relationships can be overwhelming.

In addition, many autistic people have difficulty recognizing social cues, body language, and situational meanings, and this often leads to discomfort or frustration. The fact that some people like to hug presents problems for tactile-sensitive autistic people, as does understanding others' motives. For example, if an autistic person is invited to a movie, they might want to see it, so they agree. Their inviter might see the movie activity as a date and infer that acceptance of the invitation means mutual interest in each other, rather than in the movie. Thus, a whole host of misunderstandings can come from that. There's also the consideration that autistic people often mimic behaviors they see in others as a means of masking or fitting in; if someone grows up in an abusive, neglectful, or otherwise damaging environment, they might not know how to relate differently.

Last, and perhaps most important, autistic people have been trying to fit into the NT world for decades. Thus, when they have a supportive environment, they engage in lessons teaching them how to assimilate, how to treat others so as to fit in with the mainstream. Much less often are autistic people taught how people should treat them. Again, having people around is not the same as having friends, but due to ASD traits including a high tendency to cooperate (when not highly overwhelmed), the autistic person might be slow to recognize unhealthy relationships or to communicate specific needs in that area.

Lisa states:

I have a person in my life who knows what a healthy relationship looks like and who, I believe, lives with boundaries to keep her relationships healthy. Since meeting her, it's been uncomfortable for me because I don't completely understand healthy relationships quite yet. She has a heart of gold, helps other people all the time, and her career is all about helping people too. Yet, I don't understand her sometimes. I know it's because I'm waiting to be misunderstood, judged, and/or accused of something; but it doesn't happen. Instead, there's actual open communication and honest dialog between her and me. There's nothing I can do or cannot do regarding her part of this relationship, and she, I believe, only lets my part of our relationship affect her according to the strong boundaries she sets for herself. I think I'm supposed to do the same so this relationship can stay healthy and balanced. I want to understand and participate in a healthy way, yet I don't know how to do that yet by reason of so many past unhealthy relationships.

I'm used to being abused, controlled, considered worthless, and hurt. I'm used to knowing if I'm in trouble and some kind of abusive interaction is coming my way, or if I'm ok for the moment. In abusive relationships, I've been able to gauge the situation by keeping a very close eye on my abuser and being tuned in to their moods. There is no way of knowing where I stand with my new friend because her moods are independent of our interactions. She's happy most of the time anyway. But, if I keep a close eye on her when I'm with her, no matter what happens, I still don't know where I stand with her. I feel like I'm not always supposed to be focusing on where I stand with her because of trust, but I'm not comfortable with trust.

In the abusive relationships I've been in, I have had some control. When my abuser is in a certain mood, I know what to do to alleviate it or at least keep some semblance of peace. I have been able to push buttons to rile the abusive person, even if I know I'm going to get hurt. In abusive relationships I have been able to manipulate myself, the abusive person, daily challenges, or whatever I've needed to, to keep the peace. I've known by looking at my abuser what kind of day it will be for my family.

With my new friend, there's nothing I do that matters, unless, I suppose, I do something blatantly rude or hurtful, but even then, I think we'd talk about it and work it out. Her relationship with me doesn't depend on just me, it depends on both of us, and trust. So strange.

In my grief group, I have had a positive relationship with most of the women. We share similar life experiences. We also have other things in common such as difficult husbands, whether gone or still with us, the loss of important people in our lives, single parenting, loneliness, and daily struggles that seem too big sometimes. I only see them once a week for 1.5 hours in a setting that has a structured routine. We rarely text and have gotten together once in the two years since I've known them. Are those healthy relationships? Are they even relationships?

Jenna, Darci, Sylvia, and Loren—I've known all of these women for 20 to 28 years. They live in different locations in the USA. I mostly text, sometimes call them, and we've visited each other through the years. I enjoy their company and they seem to enjoy mine, but are these healthy relationships enough to keep me from feeling isolated? They are so far away. The connections come and go depending on whether I call, text, or visit them, and as always, the connection waxes and wanes.

Chapter III

Living with PTSD

What is PTSD?

In many ways, we are in control of our day via the cognitive (thinking, processing, problem-solving) and behavioral (how we act, what we do) choices resulting from what goes on in our brain. In a neurotypical brain, various systems operate according to sensory stimuli and past learning, which then produce thoughts, feelings, and actions. Activity is synchronized—different parts that do various jobs all smoothly work together (Just *et al.* 2004). Most people aren't aware of how much is going on in their head; there are things to do, places to go, pressing needs. NTs develop a schema for much of their daily operation. Schemas are like shortcuts—they develop over time and allow an NT brain to interpret lots of information very quickly, without even thinking about it. For example, an individual who works outside the home gets ready for work, finds lunch, keys, car, way to work, parking spot, door, desk, and lots of other things by schema and rote memory. The brain is doing a lot of work, but the NT is largely unaware of it. In the brain of a person having undergone traumatic experiences, however, things can work much, much differently.

Because danger and trauma are subjective perceptions, meaning they are specific to the individual, what one sees as overwhelming to coping resources, another may not. Also, one person with PTSD is not "weaker" than another who didn't develop PTSD. There are so many variables in the nature and nurture of an individual contributing to personal makeup, that researchers will be employed for decades to come.

Even within the same families, development and perceptions about upbringing are different for everyone. Social support, community support, socioeconomic situations, and a wide array of other ecological variants contribute to how the body and mind interpret each experience. Sometimes, an experience (or many) taxes one's coping capacity so severely that pathways in the brain become changed. Perceptions are shifted. Behaviors become reactive. Indeed, one man with PTSD who did not recognize it for many years after returning from war describes it as follows:

> PTSD reminds me of an evil thief who tries to steal everything from you—your life, your family, and your mind. It won't let you get close to people. It eats you alive from the inside out. PTSD has no mercy and its only goal is to devour your mind, body, and spirit. It's a beast that never sleeps. (Martinez 2015)

I. Criteria/causes

A diagnosis of PTSD is recognized via criteria put forth in the *DSM-V* (APA 2013), with consideration for differential diagnoses. In general, a person needs to experience, and either physically or vicariously witness, an incident or incidences wherein their person felt threatened by imminent death, sexual violence, or serious injury. An event is key. Stemming from this are symptoms such as having flashbacks wherein the person sees, smells, hears, and feels as if the incident is actually occurring again. They might be constantly on guard, jumpy, or expecting the worst. They might avoid reminders such as the site of an accident, family members, dark basements, cold nights, certain music, or even sweets. They might get angry quickly and have trouble getting themselves back to baseline. They may have attention and concentration troubles. Their body doesn't always work right. Sleep issues are common. Relationships can be hard. Substance use is not an uncommon way to avoid feelings or memories.

For certain, the anxiety they feel is not "just" an occasional increase in worry; it's intense, overwhelming, unpredictable, constant, confusing, and painful. People with PTSD often don't trust themselves or others. On the one hand, they might know their perceptions are off, but on the other, that's all they've got to rely on. And feelings, memories, and fear can come from nowhere. Indeed, research has demonstrated that many parts of the brain are affected, and neural pathways are altered.

Brain changes after trauma

Given various brain development at various ages, trauma has different effects at different ages. The brain has compensating ability in some situations but not others. Nurturing, too, affects resilience. In short, every brain works differently, within a complicated but smoothly running framework...unless epigenetics, injury, or trauma occur.

In the present discussion there are three structures within the brain of particular interest. First, the amygdala, which is a small, almond-sized structure that stores emotion memory and is also connected with basic responses like touch, smell, pain sensitivity, and breathing. It is also the conductor of the "fight-or-flight" response. As such, the amygdala is strongly associated with emotional processing, including fear-learning. Fear-learning is when an organism learns to connect a seemingly innocuous stimulus (the smell of pipe tobacco, for instance) with another stimulus that is highly disagreeable and produces fear (being assaulted). In PTSD, the amygdala demonstrates super-heightened functioning. It tends to loop around and around, looking for and associating threats again and again. The increased action in the amygdala is associated with aggression, irritability, loss of emotion control, extreme startle response, disruption of short-term memory, and deficits in recognizing emotions.

A second brain structure also very sensitive to trauma is the hippocampus. It is chiefly involved in storing and retrieving memories. It also seems to help in the ability to manage fear. When a brain is chronically stressed or outright overwhelmed, the hippocampus can be damaged. This might cause someone with PTSD to have no memory of some incidents while having intense memories of others.

Lots of things happen in various parts of the brain all at once. The thalamus is chiefly responsible for integrating all that information and sending it to where it needs to go. Thus, the thalamus is strongly involved in things like perception, attention, timing, and movement. It also plays a big role in alertness and awareness. Trauma expert Bessel van der Kolk (2014) equates this structure to that of a cook, who takes all kinds of different ingredients (e.g., sensations, experience, education) and mixes them up just right to make a functional result (e.g., an appropriate understanding of what's happening). In PTSD, the thalamus isn't able to connect things so smoothly.

MaryD writes:

In the helping professions, we're taught to "meet the client where they are." That's nice. It sounds good, and many certainly have their hearts there. The problem is, the helper doesn't always know where "there" is. Because the brain's thinking parts are shut down in trauma, the logic or facts of a situation—what the patient has experienced—is their unique perception of it, of course, but not necessarily linear or logical. Parts are left out. Words aren't graspable. Drawings have no explanation. Thus, one cannot attend to what was "real." That makes no sense; "facts" did not enter the memory

logically but, rather, perceptually. And parts of memories
are sometimes available and sometimes not. So, in helping,
we wait. We give the patient time, validation of the emotion,
acceptance of the feelings. No undue pushing, no damnation,
no overt frustration. We challenge the perception, offer
alternative explanations, provide consistency and, hopefully,
hope. We accept projection, take their pain, and identify other
choices. Once the box is open, we cannot reseal it. One must
move on, through the fear and pain and loneliness, while
learning to act, think, and feel differently. We might make
safety contracts, and keep and review thought records, plan
responses, and evaluate results. With faith, we find "there"
together. Then the work becomes more proactive and we
begin down a more clearly defined path.

Treatment can initially be complicated by the fact that traumatic
experiences are so often working in the background. Breuer
and Freud (1957) are often referenced for their work on trauma
and the unconscious. They posit that traumatic memories may
be "completely absent from the patients' memory when they
are in a normal psychical state." Whether memories are in
the conscious, subconscious, or unconscious, perceptions and
lessons learned nevertheless influence everyday operations.
Indeed, as Freud and Breuer note, "memory of the trauma acts
like a foreign body."

A mid-life male having PTSD from multiple and chronic
childhood assaults writes:

I'm confused a lot. I often don't feel in control of me. I don't
really think things through; I don't have time. I'm busy
watching things. I'm busy trying to keep myself focused
instead of floating away in my head. Also, my sense of reality
is screwed up. When I tried, as a kid, to tell adults what was
happening to me, I was told to "shut up" and that what I said

"never happened." If that were true, I wondered, why did I think it had happened? I was continually denigrated for things that were happening to me, then told by others they didn't happen. Consequently, I can't make decisions—I don't trust myself. I change my mind a lot. I promise things I won't deliver. And time is not a concept I can grasp, either. It sneaks up on me. It might be 11am, but then it's 3pm, and I missed an appointment, or I'm late leaving to meet up. And I *never* finish anything either, because I lose time or I fear being open for criticism...even from myself. Another thing, I have a very warped sense of loyalty. I'm 60 years old, and I'm just learning that. I never learned healthy loyalty. I don't even really know who I'm trying to be loyal to. I was conditioned to be loyal to whoever was the loudest, meanest, most self-centered person in the situation. I learned to bond to those kinds of people. And lastly, I feel unworthy of the attachment of a loved one. That there is a difference between being loved and being used is foreign to me. I never learned the parts of an equitable relationship or friendship.

Consider, too, the following poem:

First chance for help

How could you walk away from me?
How could you see me in need and just turn around?
But you didn't just turn around, did you?
You closed the door behind you.
You turned around and closed the door
While he was hurting me.
I was so scared
Not the normal spook
The kind of scared were your brain takes a few seconds to decide on danger
Fight or flight

Life or death
Your mind makes the decision
Will you sink or will you swim?
A few seconds
One
Two
Three
And you won't even notice it before it just takes over
The drumroll starts inside my chest
And the other instruments kick in
Now I feel the vibrations
The symphony rattles my rib cage which causes a ripple
effect to my toes and around my skull
Now I'm drowning
I feel the water in lungs
I fumble to find the door knob, I find one, and swing myself
into the closet.
Fight or flight
Life or death
I heard you screaming downstairs, slamming the cabinets,
slamming the chairs, screaming
I crunch my body as curled up as I can get it, and try to
remember the layout of the house and where the exits are
Can I make it out?
But now the drum sticks are frozen, along with the water in
my lungs. I can't move
Fight or flight
Life or death

Flynn

The above passage and poem include a number of symptoms
that people with PTSD find themselves living with every single
day. The next section describes various indicators of PTSD.
While the list is clear, their manifestation often is not. In addition,

different people show different aspects of those symptoms, as well as various intensities.

II. Symptoms

With brain changes in mind, it may be useful to deconstruct the theoretical concept of PTSD and discuss what it looks like in daily life. But first, it is important to realize that those suffering from PTSD aren't experiencing a simply higher than normal stress response; it's much more than that. Unfortunately, the term PTSD can get thrown around irresponsibly. While high anxiety and related diagnoses are also quite painful and can interrupt life processes, PTSD is in a category all its own.

Experiences and event(s)

Most humans have a natural will to live, in body and mind. We're born with certain instincts, such as grasping and rooting reflexes, that aid in seeking safety and nutrients. As we grow, we learn things that contribute to our sense of safety and survival. Unfortunately, many also learn about things that detract from those senses. Experiencing or witnessing assaults on the body like rape, molestation, vehicular accidents, mass violence, kidnap, and critical illness, among others, can leave a person feeling betrayed by expectations of safety, nurturing, and self-determination. People can also find themselves in natural disasters like floods, tornadoes, landslides, and blizzards whereby they perceive great danger with no chance to control their living or dying.

Whatever the reason, the short version of human response is that the amygdala and its accompanying structures engage to tell all the other parts what needs to happen—survival. Hormones are released and the heart beats faster, pumping blood away from the extremities and towards organs and big muscles. Things tense up and the body braces to either fight or run. We might also freeze; like a deer caught in a car's headlights, we feel paralyzed. Some people also report dissociating—or mentally going away from the situation—only to re-associate with no memory of the "time away."

Different people handle different dangers in different ways, according to the degree of coping assets they have available at the time. All three responses—fight, flight, and freeze— have anthropological uses. Cognitively though, we don't get to choose. If the fear is great enough, lasts for a long time, or is frequent, coping mechanisms may not be enough. The brain and body learn different (often maladaptive) ways of functioning with the goal of dealing with danger.

Re-experiencing

In real life, the re-experiencing aspects of PTSD include flashbacks and nightmares. Both phenomena are generally unanticipated and debilitating. Nightmares, for example, can seem so real, and the reactions during the dream can be just as intense. Some people wake up to find themselves hiding in a closet, drenched in sweat, crying or clawing, or running down the street. Some wake up unable to move, paralyzed. Many avoid sleeping, especially at night.

Flashbacks are similar. Anything can bring them on. Though nobody is totally aware of exactly everything that's going on in a situation, the unconscious aspects of the mind often register things as a matter of course, and they might come out later. Thus, the buzzing of a bee could bring back the experience a little girl had in the back field; the smell of gasoline takes a man right back to the deadly crash; the concept of time can cause a person to feel they're right back on the hill—waiting and watching as awful things unfold.

These flashbacks aren't necessarily linear stories; sometimes they're just short flashes accompanied by reactive responses and great discombobulation. Playgrounds and bullies, basements and tornadoes, anything can be connected as transporters, triggering great fear, anger, and survivalist reactions.

The fearful places that our senses can take us to are experienced as if something is currently happening—the patient flees, or lashes out, or stays deadly still. The face of a loved one or other helper could be replaced by that of the aggressor. The patient or helper can get physically or emotionally hurt, even killed, as a result of a flashback. What they see, what they smell, what they hear, feel or taste...it's all real again in that moment. They sometimes lose track of where they are or who they're with. After the episode ends, which can be minutes, hours, or longer, the body is exhausted. The brain is spent. And there can be a lot to clean up, figuratively and literally.

Lisa shares:

> PTSD robs me of any peace or sense of safety in my present daily life and forces me to fight for my future as I mentally wrestle reliving the traumatic experiences of my past. It is insidious and can hijack my day at lightning speed upon hearing a certain sound, seeing a person or place, or smelling a triggering smell. Once the flashback has started, the damage has been done. The experience comes back so vividly, it's truly as if I've re-lived it again, only there's no one there. No one to fight off, scream at, run away from, or call the authorities on—only the feeling of an assault, the intense fear, any guilt about it I carry around, and the emptiness of going through it all alone through my thoughts. I'm left to work through all the trauma that was brought back to my conscious thoughts again. The feelings of trauma are stuck with me.

Avoidance

The intensity and surprise aspect of re-experiencing are major reasons why a patient tries, either consciously or unconsciously, to avoid reminders of the trauma. For example, a person may never go to a restaurant or wear certain shoes again; they may avoid songs or a part of town; they may collect food so as to avoid hunger; they may never attend a concert, handle money, or swim again. Irritation and angry explosions are common as these can be effective in releasing anguish and keeping others away. Some may refuse to leave their room for fear of being triggered. Indeed, even in everyday occurrences, a person with PTSD may appear to struggle or "fight" against a helper. Loved ones report seemingly simple things like suggesting a picnic or painting a room can produce tension and refusal.

Interestingly, avoidance reinforces itself. By avoiding people, places, and things that cause high anxiety, the anxiety is lessened. The more one avoids, the less anxiety is experienced. The next time a potential threat enters the person's life, they move further away and anxiety is again reduced, for the time being. Many of these responses are, at least initially, without real choice or awareness. And they interrupt regular daily, hourly, and minute routines. Family estrangement often occurs.

For example, a young adult writes:

I'm a woman. I was taught to suck it up. I don't rock the boat. I don't make other people uncomfortable. I was never allowed to quit. I got hurt, assaulted, raped, abused, and exploited, and then I got up and went to school the next day. I "fake it," but I'm sure I never actually "make it." I have to prepare myself for everything I do outside of my house. I never just "stop by" a grocery store. I have to plan for it. Days before. I only go to places I know, and if there are too many people, I put down my stuff and leave. I avoid crowds— street fairs, parades, concerts. A dark movie theater? No way.

Telephone? Rarely, and on my terms. Weddings, funerals? Nope. I know so much of my fear looks unreasonable to others. That's another reason to remain invisible.

Negative mindset

This refers to negative thoughts and mood. Indeed, patients often believe that expecting something bad to occur helps to avoid bad results. They try to be ready for not if, but when, the next danger appears. And because they have experienced dreadful things, they generally have negative thoughts about themselves or others ("I am stupid/should have known better," "I'm useless," "they're untrustworthy"). Poor memory and concentration issues feed into the denigrating mindset. Many report feeling emotionally numb. Most of those can't name more than basic emotions, if any at all. There is a lack of trust for themselves, others, and the world in general. Patients often can't imagine the future. Indeed, imagination and creativity are generally restricted to scary experiences and survival. The patient with PTSD may also have trouble with positive experiences or feelings. Many report that positive things make them feel vulnerable, with a sense of inevitable loss.

Lisa shares:

> I can't take compliments. They hurt. Compliments cause strong emotions and physical pain for me. I feel unworthy of compliments, even if they are true to the person giving them. If I have done something well, and someone tells me I did well, I want to flee. It's scary. I'm not great at naming emotions, but I know there's a bunch of them that come to the surface when I receive a compliment. It becomes overwhelming and I feel the same way, if not worse, as I would feel if someone was insulting me.
>
> Another example is that I find myself interpreting

ambiguous information in a negative way. So, if someone says hello to everyone in the group but me, I automatically begin to think things like that I've done something wrong, I'm unwelcome, and/or I'm about to be rejected. Thinking like that seems to keep me safe because as I'm looking for the shunning, I'm planning for how to handle it. That the person might have had many things on their mind or felt overwhelmed by their day, thus simply overlooked me is not a possibility I can entertain. It's too dangerous. Something might happen to surprise me and I fear I won't react well.

Arousal

Because parts of the brain are misfiring in PTSD, both brain and body are in a continual state of arousal. Hypervigilance is a term often used to describe the constant scanning of the environment—much of which is done outside of awareness. Mental processing may be slow or super-fast. Because the individual is always "on," they may cope in ways that seem odd to an outsider. For example, rather than walking between cars, they might walk the perimeter of a parking lot to their car, parking far away from any others. If someone goes to a park and it "doesn't feel right," they leave. Parents with PTSD might watch their child's sports games from far up in the seating where they can see absolutely everything. Others may move furniture in front of the doors at night. A popping balloon may send someone to the ground. The smell of a particular flower could produce unbelievable fear and paralysis. Or perhaps there is no feeling, only scanning and reacting. Sleep is poor. Fatigue is chronic. Guilt and shame are constant. It's often difficult to be productive when battling PTSD symptoms, and working outside the home may be impossible. People with PTSD often find living in a neurotypical mainstream to be painful and overwhelming.

Others may perceive innocuous remarks as threatening. Some jump when another turns the page in a book. Mood swings are common, as is rigid, either/or thinking. Anger arises here, too. Even a simple conversation can be draining as each statement is analyzed. Irritability and snapping are common. Fatigue is chronic. They never know where the threat will come from yet may be poised for action, feeling constantly overwhelmed and ineffective. Although they are constantly scanning, they are nevertheless easily spooked. Though the hypervigilant person might know they overanalyze people and environments, the results imagined should they cease their vigilance only produce greater fear rather than relaxation. It interrupts all aspects of life.

Lisa writes:

PTSD symptoms have taken over my life. They disrupt my waking life and haunt my sleep. I'm constantly waiting for something bad to happen and feel like I'm always ready to run if I need to, which is exhausting.

I experience flashbacks when a smell, thought, place, or anything that relates to a past trauma brings me back to the incident as if it just happened. It is so terrifyingly real. I have to do a lot of self-care to bring myself back to normal after a flashback. Sometimes, due to not recognizing my emotions, I don't realize I'm having a flashback and those can take forever—sometimes days and days—to work through. Once, I was triggered in the afternoon, and felt increasingly bad, anxious, and wrong all through the evening until around 11pm when I realized I had been triggered earlier that day. I have a visual memory and I see in pictures, which, I believe, intensifies my flashbacks. They are so realistic because of the way my mind works. The flashbacks come quickly and with enough strength to bring my anxiety way up, causing tears, and I feel like nothing is ok. I perseverate on the memories and the negative thoughts that follow, although I try to shift my thinking in a positive direction.

I have difficulty sleeping because I have recurring nightmares. The nightmares I have can stay with me for the whole day after I wake up and/or for several days later. The nightmares are lucid. I feel the nightmares as if I'm really experiencing them. I have senses that I'm aware of during my nightmares. I can feel touch, including pain, I can see and hear, of course, but I can also smell. The nightmares can leave me with the feeling that I actually lived through what I dreamt about—in real life—which makes me feel very bad about myself. I may have had to defend myself and what happened in the nightmare affects me as if I really experienced the violence of an attack on my life and how I handled it.

Anxiety is a constant part of my life. I go to sleep anxious, have nightmares, and wake up anxious. I worry about normal events of the day, relationships, a job, my car, my kids, my health, my kids' health, whether I'm feeding us healthy meals, what I've said, what I haven't said, if I have to go somewhere, if I stay home too much, and I could go on and on and on. I feel like I am always "on" and can never relax.

Anxiety also sits heavy on my chest to the point where sometimes it's painful and other times it's a lot of pressure. I have a lump in my throat that won't go away. My stomach hurts. My muscles are tight all day and even when I'm sleeping my jaw is so tense my teeth are sometimes loose in the morning. I feel shaky inside and sometimes that can turn into shaking on the outside as well.

III. Treatment
Differential diagnoses
Some believe that super-dangerous or near-death experiences

routinely cause PTSD. This is definitely not the case. For example, according to the US National Center for PTSD (Galovsky 2016), approximately five in ten men and six in ten women will experience a trauma in their lifetime. However, only about 4 percent of US men and 10 percent of US women develop PTSD in their lives (U.S. Department of Veterans Affairs 2019). In addition, recent research in the UK reveals PTSD in approximately 3.7 percent of men and 5.1 percent of women (Baker 2018). Thus, when clients report life trauma, it is important to consider a range of other possibilities apart from PTSD. Traumatic events can also precipitate depression, anxiety, and adjustment disorders. One might see phobias, personality changes, schizophrenia, or neurological damage, as well (NCCMH 2005). Symptoms from many of these diagnoses can appear similar to the symptoms of other conditions. Personality disorders are often confused with PTSD. Considering differential diagnoses is imperative when suspecting PTSD, because mental health and medical treatments—and the results thereof—depend on accurate assessment.

Co-occurring disorders

In co-occurring disorders, patients "have two [or more] primary, chronic, biological mental illnesses, each requiring specific treatment" (Minkoff 2001). PTSD often comes with co-occurring disorders. For example, substance use disorders and/or addictions are quite common, as are agoraphobia, generalized anxiety, panic, major depression, obsessive-compulsive disorder, and personality disorders; indeed, there is a myriad of possible co-occurring conditions that combine with individual perception, social, and medical perspectives, as well as serving to complicate experiences and outcomes.

Treating a co-occurring diagnosis is tricky, too, because while one form of intervention works with some symptoms, it might work against others. For example, while a cognitively challenged person might benefit from having a caseworker to help with housing, transportation, or medical care, that same patient might have another mental disorder that includes paranoia, and a strange person coming into their "business" might upend current stability. In these cases, treatment must focus on both things at the same time. This presents more intense challenges because what helps in one diagnosis (a caseworker for cognitive support) will likely harm in another (discombobulation due to the dynamics surrounding strangers in the home—a space regarded to be safe); nevertheless, both problems need to be honored, at the same time that the client is living all other aspects of his or her life.

Talk therapies are useful in many instances. Face-to-face interactions offer the oft-important tangible, soulful connection, where tone and body language are crucial to gaining tolerance of emotions. The telling can assist in cognitive restructuring, where one learns to view the events in a more objective way. It can help introduce us to the issues of blame, shame, and guilt. Indeed, logic combined with emotional maturity is imperative in the growing of wisdom and lasting growth. Thus, the scariest work is for the client to learn to tolerate the feeling of being terrified—flashbacks are not often predictable. Emotions come out when they do. They don't happen between 9am and 5pm. Much improvement can be made via a relational approach, that is, helping the client to connect with supportive people who can help them when they need it.

Research is robust in the co-occurring areas. Unfortunately, treatment is complicated and resources are limited. Generally, the most common and most pressing subject areas are funded for examination. This is why one can find so much in terms of PTSD and substance abuse, for example. It's extremely common. Research has provided information that has contributed greatly to the development of very useful treatment programs.

Autism, however, particularly in adults and especially regarding PTSD, is woefully under-studied. Thus, there is little direction in terms of best practice. One way to begin is by exploring others' experiences.

Chapter IV

ASD Meets PTSD

Lisa shares a typical day...

My average day is fraught with internal struggles. For example, after a restless night with nightmares and little sleep, I wake up anxious. I know the nightmares weren't real, but they seem so vividly real while I'm experiencing them, it's hard to shake off the feelings the nightmares evoked. I have to start reminding myself right away that it was just a nightmare, try to get my anxiety down, and start things I have to get done that day. If that doesn't work, I distract myself with word puzzles. I try to regulate my emotions. If that doesn't work, I have no choice. I just have to start my day. There's breakfast and school for the kids, phone calls, appointments, and lots of the usual mom things. But the day is peppered with a sensory onslaught of smells, noises, textures, and emotions, many of which trigger traumatic memories. Triggers can come at anytime from anywhere and result in flashbacks that disrupt me for a period of time I don't have to spare. It can become difficult to make decisions about where to go and what to avoid. It took me forever to decide if I could make it to the store later in the day. I couldn't go. The nightmares came again that night. I woke up, went to church and was bombarded with stimulation. Then we were invited out for lunch, which was a necessary social event for the boys. So, we went, and there was too much noise, too much conversation, too much of everything. The boys enjoyed it though. And I couldn't get to the store again. I feel like I'm in a constant state of emotional dysregulation, anxiety, no energy, and always hypervigilant about being triggered.

I. Similar symptoms

Outwardly, there appear to be similar symptoms between ASD and PTSD. Indeed, there are communication problems, perception challenges, and social skills deficits in each classification. Recognizing this, researchers recently engaged in case studies (again with children) comparing ASD with PTSD as a means of differentiating the two or finding an overlap (Stavropoulos, Bolorian and Blacher 2018). Findings suggest overlap in areas related to lack of emotional sharing, lack of interest towards peers, emotional outbursts, sleep problems, and repetitive behaviors. Interestingly, however, while the behaviors themselves look similar, the *reasons* for them may be quite different. This is important. Content matters when helpers are trying to decide how to engage the patient in managing or shifting maladaptive behaviors.

For example, in looking at *failure regarding shared emotions*, we see different reasons in each group: in PTSD, this often happens because of a reduction in positive emotions, emotional numbing, hopelessness, or avoiding emotional pain. However, in ASD, there is a deficit in social communication as emotion is difficult to recognize at all. Next, facial expressions, voice tone, and nuances of communication are also important to consider in each diagnosis as they are generally a mystery to ASD people; yet, in PTSD, those aspects are important to understanding or avoiding the perceived current threat. Then, *emotional outbursts/ implosions* are also seen in both groups. In PTSD, it can be due to extreme irritability and anger likely caused by being in a constant state of fight-or-flight, while ASD people tend to be reacting to a rigid need for routine that is not happening. *Sleep difficulties*, too, are caused by recurring nightmares (PTSD) or a neurological aspect (ASD). Lastly, showing a lack of interest in peers could be due to social withdrawal (PTSD) or deficits in social communication (ASD). The question in treatment, therefore, would be whether the goals are sufficient for the underlying reason, rather than for the behavior only.

In our work together, we have come up with a list of possible shared symptomology of PTSD in people with ASD (see Table 4.1).

Table 4.1 PTSD and ASD: often shared symptomology

PTSD	Symptom	ASD
Emotional fear elicited from real or innocuous stimuli	Avoiding	Overstimulation
Inability to attend to present moment— due to flashbacks, hypervigilance, painful memories	Working memory issues	Inability to attend to present moment—due to hyperstimulation
Painful, fearsome	Memories	May be unreliable because of focus on exact details or interest in specific details rather than overall experience
Misinterpretation; negative outlook; fear of ambiguity	Altered cognition and mood	Confusion; overload; fear of sudden, changed routine
Hyperarousal features; survival instinct; lack of early emotional training	Emotional outbursts and implosions	Rigid need for routine; difficulty switching attention; alexithymia; frustration with feeling unheard
Trouble falling asleep and recurring nightmares; hypersomnolence from medication; excessive worry; substance use	Poor sleeping	Trouble falling and staying asleep, medication side effects; spinning thoughts

cont.

PTSD	Symptom	ASD
Lack of self-confidence; low/no trust in others	Isolation	Low social skills, communication difficulties, and high desire to please can bring exploitation/confusion
Hypervigilance; flashbacks	Exhaustion	Overcompensation; masking; constant high stimulation
Sleep issues; body pain; digestive issues; sexual dysfunctions; reduced immune protection	Somatic issues	Sleep issues; body pain; digestive issues
Desire to escape pain or causing pain to others; emptiness; co-occurring mental health problem; + See everything above	Suicidal ideation/ attempts	Desire to stop the pain, hyperstimulation; co-occurring mental health problem + See everything above

Table 4.1 demonstrates how behavioral intervention programs may find some success in managing behaviors that are deemed problematic in the mainstream. It identifies specific behavioral targets to change. This can be done via addressing the context of the behavior. However, by attending only to the behavioral aspect, professionals and other helpers miss perhaps more appropriate and less time-consuming ways to help patients and their situations.

For example, consider this scenario:

A young autistic student started a new school, with a new schedule, teachers, students, and rooms. The student was doing well with all the changes, except for her daily emotional breakdown. Every morning, at 10am, the student would become inconsolable. Her outburst would disrupt the classroom. No one knew what was causing the behavior, because she seemed content and happy during the rest of her day. The teachers and aides tried different interventions, including operant conditioning, reworking her schedule, and taking the clock out of the classroom, but nothing worked. The staff were more focused on making her behaviors stop for the good of the classroom, treating them as if she was being difficult, instead of looking at her behaviors as a form of communication. Finally, someone from her new school thought to contact her old school to find out a bit more about how her days had been there. They found an important piece of information. In the student's day, right around 10am, she had a half hour block of time to work her muscles in the occupational therapy room. The staff implemented "muscle time" at her new school, which stopped all behaviors during the 10am timeframe and the problem was solved.

For many autistic students, their behaviors are corrected and/or modified to try and fit into the school society they are part of, instead of the school searching for an out-of-the-box solution that could take much less time and trauma. All behavior is communication. For the autistic student who needed muscle time but couldn't communicate that, the costs of the original interventions were confusion, being misunderstood, enduring operant conditioning, as well as, for a long time not getting the sensory stimulation she needed to be successful in her classroom.

In short, it seems that the mainstream wants autistic people with PTSD to fit into their idea of "normal," instead of the mainstream meeting them at least in the middle. Thus, with many autistic client interventions, the behavior targets are typically designed to fit into the mainstream, that is, to make the mainstream comfortable with the "problem" person, regardless of what the intervention costs the client in losing their sense of self. Hence, it may not be what the client needs, but rather what tends to help mainstream people feel comfortable with the person who has the diagnosis, instead of helping the client to work with who they really are. This problem is difficult enough when there is one serious mental health diagnosis. Having two co-occurring diagnoses creates a more complicated, more confusing, less supported, and higher-risk situation.

II. Smash-up

Another use for Table 4.1 is to demonstrate that each diagnosis in itself presents an exceptionally difficult way to live and move in the mainstream. When they occur together, the energy and coping skills are taxed exponentially.

Lisa shares:

> I experienced sudden, alarming symptoms one morning, and under the advisement of my primary care physician, I went to the ER. I was put into a room and left there for a while. No one told me what was going to happen. I couldn't ask. I had no energy left for it. I used all my energy just having the symptoms, driving there, filling out paperwork, and thinking about my doctor's reaction to my symptoms (go to the ER).
>
> The tests I had to go through at the emergency room were triggering. I was triggered by one test in a way that caused me to relive an assault I went through and I wanted to run away, but couldn't. Another test, taken right after that one, required an IV and involved being enclosed in a place I didn't want to be in. I wanted to scream, but I had to smile and thank the technician.
>
> I was then referred to a specialist. At the specialist's office, I had met her for less than five minutes before she was preparing me for a painful medical procedure that she insisted I have done right then and there based on the records from the ER. It was traumatic and painful; not only was the test itself awful, but it was sprung on me without discussion and I didn't have time to process what was happening...very similarly to how an assault happened years earlier. The procedure is usually done under planned

conscious sedation, but the doctor wanted to do the procedure immediately. The invasiveness and pain were triggering. It all happened too fast for me to process enough to advocate for myself. I tried to, but I wasn't successfully heard. The doctor had someone come in to stand beside me to distract my attention away from what was happening and to watch for a signal from me that I could not continue. Once the procedure started, I tried to be cooperative. I masked the pain and triggering. It didn't matter how badly it hurt; I was not going to say a word in order to get it over with as fast as possible.

It is essential for me to understand and acknowledge my needs. I'm in charge of my own well-being. I need time to prepare when things are going to happen to me. I need to keep my sense of autonomy. In addition to my needs due to past trauma, I also need to address the hypersensitivity piece of what's going to happen—sights, smells, noises, light, texture, colors, voice cadence, and so much more. This time I tried to advocate for myself. But, sadly, I had no validation. The doctor had a counter answer for each of my fears and anxieties, and exactly what had been planned by her happened regardless of what I said. Things were going fast, and I was processing slow.

In her trauma work, Lisa has been presented with situations that have challenged her in both diagnoses, simultaneously, eliciting symptoms that interrupt successful outcomes. The quandary has been how to approach a symptom, such as avoidance, on the whole, while also attending to individual context—at the same time trying not to increase distress on one end for the sake of the other. For example, when trying to address avoidance behavior, one complication for Lisa is her desire to be cooperative while also protecting herself. So, she might be invited to a holiday occasion where there will be a person who has hurt her.

She will be expected to interact with that person, which taxes not only the ASD aspects of communication, but the PTSD parts that leave her feeling powerless. The behavior is the same—avoidance—but the contexts are different. They are opposing drives. Does Lisa work on finding a safe way to integrate herself so as to improve her communication skills and participate in an important holiday ritual, as she is expected to, or does she work on physical safety at the expense of integration and cooperation? When faced with such confusing choices, negative thinking comes into play, too, in that she is certain she will not make "the right" choice, which will lead to difficult consequences. Choices like this, between antagonizing components, can leave her feeling hopeless. No matter what she tries, it will take days to process and recover.

Another event where competing needs came into play was when Lisa was giving a speech at a national conference. Because she has a high desire to educate open minds on ASD in real life, she worked for months on a very personal, enlightening speech about living with autism. As she did so, memories came up that she hadn't expected, and they were very unpleasant. She was on a deadline, having made a fixed (rigid) decision to present the speech (as she agreed to do), with a memory full of terrible things, trying to make sense of them, while experiencing sights, sounds, and smells from both the original trauma and the current environment. The ASD part provided sensory experiences in the present time while the PTSD brought sensory experiences in years past as though they were happening now, too. Her self-confidence and trust were wrecked, but she didn't know it. Her body hurt. She was hard on herself, as others had been in her earlier life. Time was of the essence, yet she lost a lot of time. She was unable to recognize or communicate her needs. The ASD also made it hard to perceive the emotions, and both the rigidity of routine and the never-ending environmental sensitivity didn't allow her to "take the day off" to take care of herself. Indeed, one of the major aspects of Lisa's particular constellation of symptoms (as it is with many ASD people), is that she doesn't understand how to "let go" of something that isn't tangible.

Though the two incidents above are special situations that may not be experienced by autistic people very often, the clashing of symptoms happens in ordinary situations as well.

For example, in the writing of this book, confusion sometimes paused the process. In one paragraph, MaryD wrote that Lisa has "natural empathy." Empathy, to Lisa, is a "good" trait, so this is where the smash-up happens: Lisa got caught up in that description of herself because a) though she feels very deeply and can be emotionally burdened with other people's anguish, she cannot say she is a "natural" because there is no quantifiable evidence (ASD); and b) she continually has trouble saying or accepting good things about herself because her mind has been coerced into believing "bragging" about herself will cause interpersonal adversity. The fear is greater than the truth (PTSD).

Thus, in accepting her strengths, Lisa is often caught between no evidence for what she knows, and finding it easier to deny good things in favor of perceived safety. Something a non-autistic person might consider "easy" can take several hours or even days of thinking and feeling for the autistic individual with PTSD before they can move forward with confidence.

Lisa continues:

> I know that ASD/PTSD also smash together in situations where professionals are trying to help me. One way that I have noticed is that of negative interpretations. In PTSD, my brain tries to keep me safe by finding possible danger. Because I've been hurt in many different ways, my brain can find danger in the smallest of ways: slight body movements, a facial muscle move, an awkwardly asked question, being left out of acknowledgment in a crowd, yelling (even if it

isn't towards me), TV shows, billing statements crossing in the mail, or someone being short in their responses, just to name a few. Until just a few years ago, I had always found it easier to be quiet, take blame, anticipate others' needs (real or imagined), and doubt myself at every turn. My PTSD symptoms can be triggered without warning, and I'm just learning what are danger perceptions and what is real. This gets complicated by the ASD rigidness wherein I need things to be predictable and consistent. The ASD makes it challenging for me to imagine others' mindsets; I read people according to what they present in the moment, rather than what they might be going through internally. I see what I see and I make judgments about my safety in the moment.

So, for example, once, when my son's support person said, "Good job, Mom," I felt patronized, since I am so often in the public social world. I became overwhelmed with feelings of injustice, anger, and distrust. I felt the need to flee, because I was experiencing multiple emotions. It is a difficult concept for me to recognize in the moment that the support person might have been saying that to benefit my son, who needs to see adults get along and his mother as knowing the score. I can't find the words to communicate; I'm often at a loss for identifying emotions. So often, instead of hearing that a problem exists, I hear someone blaming me for the problem, and my mind goes to me being less-than and just not enough. I can easily feel unvalued and misunderstood. It doesn't always occur to me that I myself misunderstand. Safety is paramount. I cling to past "lessons" because that's what I know, and because I believe that they will keep me safe. I don't know which cognitive experiences are true, and which are due to PTSD.

Another way in which PTSD and ASD tend to smash together is in other people's preconceived notions about my brain. In surface communications with people who are not regularly a part of my life, I tend to not disclose myself as autistic. It's too complicated. I try to mask and move through the various experiences. I can still get hurt and often times very confused, but I keep it to myself and try to process it on my own. There have been times when I have had to reveal myself, however. Sometimes, such as with a doctor or with school system officials, I cannot get myself understood and so I have to explain that I'm autistic and my mind interprets things differently from the mainstream. I share my diagnosis in the hope that they will be open to working with my neurology as well as theirs. Sometimes, that works out well. Other times, it does not. What I'm asking for here is presumed competence. I'm different in some ways from mainstream people, but I'm not an anomaly and I'm certainly not stupid. I've had to explain myself to therapists, prescribers, group leaders, even with long-term relationships—people I'd think might know better. But not everyone does. I've had people begin speaking in high volume, as if I'm deaf. I've had people try to explain away their ill-informed behavior. I have people explain other people to me. What I often *don't* have is people trying to understand me and my neurology. I feel continually undermined and discredited. And while I'd love to cut people like that some slack, I can't always do that because the situation often doesn't make any sense. Here's a story that might help with understanding this:

> A mother and her child's clinician were talking amiably, when all of a sudden, after the mother explained a situation with her son to the clinician, he reacted in a confusing way. He got up in his seat, and leaned forward towards the mother with a look on his face that was not friendly. The clinician then demanded he was right because "he is the clinician," and he continued to tell the mother how she was wrong.

The mother never saw the situation as right or wrong; her fight-or-flight reaction had kicked in and she found herself stuck in the seat unable to move, likely both due to her slow processing of what was happening (ASD) and the triggers she was experiencing (PTSD.) The autistic mother could no longer hear what was being said, and the clinician seemed far away, as she began to dissociate (PTSD). She eventually said she needed to go and left, so her child and his clinician could talk. She was overwhelmed but needed to keep it together for her child.

After the session, the clinician asked to see the mother again. She complied, because she was somehow compelled to do what he asked of her (ASD). The clinician tried to explain what happened, including the time he reacted aggressively, but the mother found she couldn't make sense of his words; she was on hyper alert, watching his hands, listening for tone, waiting for reactions (PTSD), and she had so many thoughts swirling around she couldn't find the proper words (ASD). The mother told the clinician she was confused, and so he tried to explain it in a different way. The clinician used metaphors, which were perplexing to her (ASD). The mother was still confused, because the word "confused" doesn't mean she needed his words explained to her in a different way. It meant she was in a state of bewilderment and uncertainty about what had happened earlier. She felt like she could neither go forward to resolution, nor backward to review the event.

The mother went away from the clinician's office feeling very misunderstood, confused, frustrated, intimidated, defeated, and triggered. The clinician didn't understand her autism, even though he was aware of it. She was triggered and struggled for the rest of the day, while fighting off bad thoughts, to figure out where it all went wrong in the clinician's room, and thinking about how she could possibly protect herself at next week's appointment, which she categorically wanted to avoid.

Another kind of situation in which all my symptoms mesh together is friendships. Although I have trouble recognizing my own emotions and communicating them, I am able to feel other people's emotional pain. I am naturally an empath and apparently, I'm easy to talk to. (Note: Talking *to* someone is different than talking *with* someone.) I listen well. When friends or even strangers feel comfortable enough to tell me their sadness or pain, I tend to feel it with them. That way my symptoms smash-up comes into play here, too, because I am sometimes triggered by the emotions I feel and start reliving abusive experiences from my past. I can't identify the feelings I might get, I can't communicate the need for help, and it can take an awfully long time to process that someone else's experience really isn't mine although I felt their pain. I can't move away from people who are essentially passing their pain onto me unwittingly. While self-care is very important, and it might help me if I stopped listening, I'd feel too badly later on for walking away. I can't seem to take care of myself if it means not "helping" another person, in other words, putting my own needs before theirs. I get confused between the past abuse that had me believing I am unworthy and that any concern for myself is selfish (PTSD), and the cooperative, desire-to-please part of me (ASD) that is driven to help.

Someone might say, for instance, that they are overwhelmed and are going to take a break for self-care. I admire that boundary they set for themselves. I'm still not in a place where I could help myself in lieu of helping someone else. Unfortunately for me, there is still the lingering feeling of being judged somehow for being selfish, and the strong desire to not make any waves or give any reason to be rejected.

One thing people say to an empathic autistic person about how they hold on to others' pain is that they should "let go" of it. For many, the ASD brain doesn't understand this concept. How can someone let go of something that they don't have in their hand? Whatever it is that people think they should "let go" of should be tangible, right? Otherwise, when they open their hand, nothing happens.

MaryD writes:

It took a while for me to correct how many phrases I use that are not literal, and I'm still learning. There are a lot, and they complicate things for ASD folk. For example, in my work, I tend to teach a lot. People often will feel embarrassed by not knowing something they feel they "should" know. My response for a while was, "Where did you pick it up?" This then often led to discussion about how one often can't know what one isn't taught one way or another. Early on in my work with ASD clients, I used such a phrase with one woman who was autistic. I didn't ask her more accurately how she learned the skill, at what developmental age one might learn the skill, or who might or might not have taught it to her. So instead of having a discussion addressing self-denigration and things she felt were lacking in her skill set, we were having two different conversations; she felt confused about not knowing what thing to "pick up" or where it was, and I was frustrated with myself for multiple failed interventions. It took her three weeks to tell me that she just couldn't figure out what to pick up. I learned to scrutinize my vocabulary because, as she so often told me (but I didn't understand), "words have meaning."

A similar situation happened with Lisa, when I asked her, "What's your weekend look like?" Her response was, "Two purple rectangular boxes, one for Saturday and one for Sunday." That's how she saw it, and that's exactly what I asked.

Indeed, literalness is a huge issue for ASD people, as Lisa shares:

I remember a time from my childhood, there was a girl in a nearby neighborhood whose mother yelled at her a lot. The girl yelled right back, and at times she would run away to school or the park. One day, as I was passing by her house, I heard her mother scream, "I'm going to kill her!" I was very worried for the girl, who I considered someone I knew, which often meant "friend." I became increasingly worried about her safety, even though later that day I saw the two of them talking amiably together.

If I weren't autistic, I might have understood that her mother's comment wasn't literal. It didn't occur to me that the statement was figurative, or said in haste, or anything else except that girl could be killed. I worried and worried which one would be dead when I passed the house again, because the girl was pretty tough, and her mother was pretty tough. I didn't know what to do and I never considered reaching out for help because that was not part of my skill set yet—I internalized everything. I didn't know what to trust, the yelling I heard from the mother, or them talking amiably together later that day. I waited for the girl after school and followed her home for a couple days in a row, just to be sure she was safe. Eventually, I saw the two of them laughing on the porch. I was really confused and agitated for many days. Still, I did not know it wasn't a literal expression; literal things like this often contributed to the accumulated trauma of my childhood. And no one knew. I didn't even really know.

It can be a social situation I don't understand. I may question why a person said what they said, or did what they did, which may have been hurtful or confusing. Typically, from most people, what I hear next is that the person is going through a difficult time (ignoring what they did that was confusing or rude to me—and ignoring the fact that I'm also going through a difficult time) and I'm told to just "not take it personally." I don't understand the apparent NT rule where if someone's going through a hard time, it's ok to be rude. It seems to me, the other person has gotten away with a social blunder that I would get completely blamed for and made out to be a bad person because of. I don't remember ever having someone say to another person on my behalf, that "she's going through a difficult time" and actually being given the benefit of the doubt by someone I may have hurt or confused. For some reason, I'm still on the hook for every social faux pas I do. I have tried, but it seems I can't understand how going through a difficult time gives a person permission to break social rules resulting in being rude and hurtful. Aren't most people going through a difficult time at some level?

III. What can cause PTSD for an autistic person?
Social relationships

Relationships of varying kinds are fraught with potentially traumatic situations for autistic adults. Due to the trouble with socioemotional reciprocity and difficulty interpreting non-verbal behaviors, communication—and any resultant bonding—is challenging. Autistic people seek routine and they focus on the details of a situation. They might have intense or specific interests and be unable to see the point of small talk; or they're direct and honest, often without value judgments as non-autistic people understand them. Thus, an autistic person might appear to a non-autistic person as discourteous, impolite, or just weird (which, of course, isn't true). Also, autistic people are often driven to understand social communication, such that interactions between people can be understood. While socializing in the mainstream world, the number of unknowns can seem boundless. Thus, when trying to "be" in a busy NT environment, autistic people can appear to need more than a mainstream person might, simply because the busy non-autistic person switches gears quickly and so, to the autistic person, speaks in an unexpected manner. Irritation, unfortunately, is put onto the neurodivergent person rather than seeing that the two people have different ways of saying the same thing. The autistic person will turn things over and over again in their mind, looking for what happened. Closure of a relationship or social situation doesn't just happen for an autistic person; they need definite information. Otherwise, thoughts and concerns keep floating around, bumping into other situations, eventually becoming mixed up and overwhelming.

Lisa writes:

Relationships are difficult for the majority of autistic people. Even as a graduate-level educated person with an above-average intelligence quotient, I can't always grasp the fundamentals involved in making, keeping, and maintaining relationships. More often than not, a person I'm in a relationship with will all of a sudden stop contact without closure or a chance to fix any mistakes I may have made, and it's usually a permanent loss. Also, the mistakes may not have even been mine, or theirs, but simply a miscommunication. It can be heartbreaking, or at the very least disconcerting.

Social support

Social support, defined here as a feeling of belongingness and being valued by others, is an important part of emotional security. In a neurotypical population, social support is an important factor in trauma experiences. Its presence can moderate or prevent a stress appraisal; it can also help victims recover more readily from the impact of a stressful event. However, social support offered from the perspective of the giver, rather than for the receiver, can be harmful. Indeed, social support from family and friends is one of the most important factors affecting the loss experience, as its presence can attenuate or prevent a stress appraisal as well as help individuals to recover more readily from the impact of a stress event (e.g., Weiss, Garvert and Cloitre 2015). Social support is defined as "the feeling of belonging to and of being esteemed by" a group perceived to be significant to a person's perception of emotional security (Keefe 1984). Research findings suggest that greater social support is related to significantly lowered levels of stress symptoms.

Social support can make or break a person. If an autistic person is already feeling fragile and they reach out for help to a support person who doesn't understand autism, they can do much more harm than help. Thus, it depends on the type of social support being offered. There are family and friends, social workers, church groups, support groups, behavioral health people, therapists, and case managers. It also depends on how much social support is available, and when.

Lisa shares:

Sometimes it helps, other times it hurts. It hurts when I have been told I have support and then suddenly it is gone. If support is offered but then what was offered never transpires, the confusion, the pain, the fear of not knowing who to count on, and of spending time trying to figure out what went wrong, is very real. The hurt is realizing the person who offered to support me—didn't. I go from a potentially hopeful situation to the old familiar aloneness—convinced I will always be alone.

The abrupt change is the first thing I wrestle with when the support is gone or never transpired. Change affects my whole life in some way or another. And change happens every day, on many levels. My anxiety heightens, I have to deal with thoughts I know are distorted, but due to so many other times of rejection, it's difficult for my heart to catch up to my head in sorting out those thoughts.

Trust is another issue that I wrestle with when my support changes suddenly, because it feels like all the other times I've been rejected, discarded, or unwanted. So, I wonder, did I interpret their offer correctly? Was the relationship even real? Why did they say they'd support me if they didn't mean it? I don't trust what I perceived. And I don't know how to fit that into future encounters with people. And, I am left alone, with no support.

One thing that is very helpful is allowing me to support myself in doing what I need to do *at the very time I need to do it*. So, for example, I was at my grief group one night and someone said something that triggered me. It took me a little bit to recognize I was having feelings and that they were really bad. I was having a flashback. I experienced sights, smells, and sounds. I couldn't concentrate. I couldn't ask for help. I had to leave the room and seek somewhere quiet, which I did. But the staff didn't know this was how to manage what I was going through. They kept coming in and out of the room, asking me if I wanted to breathe with them, if I wanted to talk to them, or if I wanted to call somebody. It was too much! There were too many words, decisions to make, and interruptions of my efforts at regulating myself, but I couldn't speak except to ask them to go away. They were doing all the things they knew to do for a non-autistic person. I just needed somewhere to lay, with a minimal amount of stimulation, until I could get myself back together. Forcing an autistic person with PTSD to fit into a neurotypical crisis treatment plan can be extraordinarily harmful to them. As shown above, between the hopeful promise of support that never transpires, and helpful people treating me as non-autistic, the best support

person for me that night was me...in the way I needed...
for me.

My reality in receiving support, as well as many others'
on the autism spectrum, is that it is not always helpful. After
experiencing unhelpful support time and time again, there's
an innate self-preservation awareness that support can be
hurtful and/or harmful. The decision becomes one of having
to choose between two unpleasant scenarios: reach out for
support, hoping someone understands autism and PTSD, or
don't reach out and be alone with no support. Both can be
equally distressing.

Abusive professional interactions/social relationships

An autistic person is vulnerable because of the social
communication difficulties inherent in autism. The resulting
misunderstandings and miscommunications are daily
occurrences, usually happening concurrently in multiples, and
become a source of alienation, rejection, and ostracization from
society. Abusive social interactions can be as seemingly mild as
a comment or as traumatic as bullying or assaults.

Imagine being on a business call where maybe two non-
autistic people and one autistic person are talking. Then, during
the call, as the majority of the conversation is taking place
between the two non-autistic people, the heart of the autistic
person with PTSD just deflates from disappointment. Though
the issue may objectively be one of cultural incompetency on
the part of the non-autistic people, the autistic person with
PTSD may easily feel that they have been presumed defective
yet again, left out of the conversation, and deemed unworthy.
Maybe they are, and they are the last person to know. Those
thoughts are immediate, along with feelings of being invisible,
less-than, and discarded. Someone needs to notice, but it can't
always be up to the client or patient to train others.

Autistic people can be taken advantage of at work because of certain characteristics of autism. A job they enjoy, where they have the skills to do the work, are highly focused, attend to details, socialize very little, and work until they are finished is a perfect setting for them, but it can go either way: they can feel effective in their work, or they can be exploited.

Lisa shares:

I worked as a computer engineer right out of college. My job was to support their CAD/CAE/CAM software, writing programs to meet specific needs for the manufacturing department. As the new hire, I would take on assignments as they were given to me while I learned the programming language they used: Rational Fortran (RATFOR).

One day, a co-worker came to my desk and said he had to go over some specifications of a program he was writing that I was going to help him finish. After that project was completed, I kept getting more and more of my co-worker's projects to do as well as mine. I tried talking to him, but he just said it came down from management. It finally got to the point where my own work was suffering. It was looking like I couldn't keep up. My co-worker either did nothing or worked on the house he was designing for himself on company time. There were even times he'd talk and talk and talk to me about his new house, keeping me from doing our work!

I went to my manager and explained to him that I couldn't do my work and the work of my co-worker. He told me I was doing a fine job, I had nothing to worry about, and that he knew how much work I was doing. I kept trying, at different times, to explain the unfairness of the situation. I got nowhere with him and was beginning to discern I was not being heard at all, but could not fathom why.

One particularly frustrating day, I went into my manager's office (cubicle) again to try to reason with him about my doing the work of two people. At one point, I raised my voice in an effort to show how frustrated I was because just talking was not working. The next thing I heard was a manager in the next office cubicle over asking my manager if he was ok. The other manager must have heard everything I was saying because there's no privacy with cubicles, yet still, he only asked my manager if he was ok. What that did was to validate my manager's stance and I lost my plea for fairness. My manager, my co-worker, and the manager from the other cubicle all let the uneven workload continue. I became confused as to what was ok and what wasn't; I had to either trust those other people or trust myself. I felt ineffective, with no one to tell and no way to increase my productivity. In reality, I was being exploited.

An autistic employee eventually comes to a place where they have to make a very difficult decision. The employee has to decide if disclosing their diagnosis will improve the quality of their work day and potentially increase their productivity or cause more distress than it's worth. It is always a gamble to disclose an autism diagnosis. There is a definite change between you and the person/people you tell. It is a decision that must be given plenty of time to mull over.

Lisa shares:

After being diagnosed in July of 2010, I was hired to teach at a private school for academically struggling students. The idea behind the school was to fill in the missing gaps in the students' education and/or social communication. The students that came to us were usually traumatized, had mental health diagnoses, and didn't trust the school staff at all. The first goal was to bring them to a place where they felt safe at the school so we could start teaching them.

Although there were only six staff members, I had trouble

with social communication right away. My supervisor would come to me with her complaints about the school leader, which made me feel very uncomfortable. They expected me to know how to handle the needs and behaviors of the students immediately, before I had time to get to know them. I had one staff member I could confide in if I had questions. The school leader would come into my classroom, witness a struggling student, and instead of helping she would just tell me I had better get my classroom under control. I kept seeing staff members walking around in the afternoon with coffee drinks that looked delicious. I watched until I figured out someone was going around taking coffee orders, but they never asked me. When I finally said something, I was told that no one knew I liked coffee. No one had asked! I thought the rule of politeness was that someone would know I was new and ask if I wanted a coffee. So I waited. It seems the rule was for me to just say I wanted coffee. I thought it would be rude for me to do that. No one was sorry for not thinking to ask the new teacher, and from then on, I was included. Simple, right? No, I had to struggle with being triggered from being left out so many other times in my life.

With all of these social communication difficulties and the sensory overload I regularly experienced with managing the students' difficult behaviors, I decided to disclose my diagnosis. I went to the school leader and told her I had received a diagnosis of Asperger's Syndrome that year, and I wanted her to know so she could understand me better.

She replied that she thought she had Asperger's Syndrome too, because "we are all on the spectrum somewhere." That statement, not backed up by any lived experience, diagnosis, or social difficulties set the tone for me: that if she could do her job, I could definitely do mine because she was the school leader with more responsibilities than I had.

What was taken away from me with that one sentence

was acceptance, understanding, assistance, and empathy, and it resulted in me continuing to socially struggle at the school. In fact, she started being more vocal about herself being on the spectrum and taking special accommodations, while I got quieter and quieter about my struggles. My supervisor also decided that "everyone was on the spectrum somewhere," which cemented the school leader's thoughts about her place on the spectrum.

Our school had at least a third of the students diagnosed as autistic. We all knew the symptoms, the ways in which autism presented, what the students needed, and how to communicate with them pretty well. No one noticed how similar I was to the students. The other teachers did comment on how well I communicated with the students and how much they communicated with me, but they never caught on as to why.

After this experience, I have been extremely careful about disclosing my diagnosis. When I have disclosed my diagnosis in situations where I feel it would make a positive difference, I continue to be misunderstood. The situations where I have chosen to disclose my diagnosis have been with people who are in the helping fields such as teachers, special education directors, nurses, doctors, behavioral health providers, and mental health providers. I choose people who I believe must be aware of autism and most likely have worked with autistic people, yet I feel I'm still not accepted as autistic. I feel either deemed to be a bad person, or looked at as an incompetent "autistic" person who is the cause of all the difficulties being addressed at the time.

Offhand comments

So, while disclosing a diagnosis could be a positive step out of the isolation of social masking and into awareness and acceptance, the interaction can also be so utterly defeating—the autistic person often does not try again.

Traumatic social interactions can be from experiencing verbal, physical, emotional, and/or sexual abuse in the home, workplace, community, school, or anywhere there are people. Many times, the bullying and abuse go unreported because the autistic person may not know what's happening to them is abusive, or they do not know the logistics of reporting to authorities, or they do report to authorities only to find no understanding or support.

There are too many scenarios to list that can result in autistic people developing PTSD, such as a comment from a misguided person saying, "Aren't we all a little autistic?", which actually completely dismisses the struggles, pain, alienation, loneliness, as well as the very difficult work of masking, exhausting confusion, and so many other conflicts and striving that go into living with autism. It can cause an autistic person enough pain that they stop choosing to disclose their autism diagnosis, which in an ideal world would help them be known for who they inherently are as a person. But that's not reality; the world is not ideal, and the different are often rejected or overlooked in response to abusive social interactions. The similarities among the scenarios are enough to understand the fundamental issues leading to abuse and ultimately to PTSD. Some of the similarities include misunderstandings, preconceived judgments, cultural differences, unaccepted differences, miscommunication, and the vulnerabilities inherent to autistic people.

Social neglect/invisibility/alone-ness

Autistic people with PTSD have to live in the same world as NTs. They may already feel confused by their world, and the less social support they have, the more prone to hurt they may become. More often than not, autistic people are quite agreeable, and are sometimes seen as pliable. PTSD, though, makes many prefer to avoid people and things. If there are partners, children, mortgages, neighbors, and so on, there is often little choice but to participate. So imagine you're a dual-diagnosis person and you have children. They need you to support them, and they like school sports. Now, imagine a nice person in front of you in a brightly lit room at your child's school. That person is a professional, or at least someone who you think probably knows more than you. They talk fast or loud or with big hand gestures. You're attending to the environment, the colors, the noise, the traffic, the temperature, and the hands. You may process language more slowly or don't understand social nuance or you're scanning the environment for threat or exit. Then you're asked to agree to something the Hand wants you to do. You're overwhelmed but want to support (or maybe you want them to stop talking), so you say yes—to what, you don't know. Suddenly, you're led to a gymnasium and placed at a table to sell raffle tickets and cookies. The gym is full—basketballs rebounding, voices yelling and bouncing off the walls. You don't know what you're supposed to do; people are in a hurry—they want their change. And their cookie. In a bag. And tickets. The buzzer is ringing. Lights are humming. Announcers talking over the loudspeaker. Singers singing. Cheerleaders cheering. OVERLOAD—fear, flee, freeze, embarrassment, humiliation, failure, alone-ness. There's too much visibility and not enough. You feel like you've failed yourself, your child, the school. What would you do differently? Who knows? You can't even remember what just happened! This was not just a misadventure. This was socially traumatic. These kinds of experiences often contribute to feelings of supreme deficiency.

Lisa shares:

> This scenario has happened to me many times while helping
> out in my sons' classrooms. There are a few I could share,

but one field trip was particularly difficult. It was in Florida, in June, which is one of the most hot and humid times of the year there. I'm sensitive to heat and humidity, which leaves me feeling sick and deflated. I have no energy, I'm distracted, and feel out of place in my own skin.

The field trip was at Marina Jacks in Sarasota. It was my day off and I went with my son's class to see billboard-sized drawings from people all over the world, and local people as well, who entered and won the contest. Marina Jacks is a peninsula-shaped park, surrounded by water on three sides. It has lots of people, playground equipment, rental boats, a restaurant, and walking paths throughout the whole park including the perimeter near the water.

When I got there, I was assigned five boys. I was told they were given to me to supervise because I was a teacher by trade and the boys were difficult to manage. The boys did not know me. They were completely uninterested in the billboards and wanted to run the walking paths, go near the water, and play on the playground equipment.

I had prepared myself for the heat and humidity, to be near and in crowds of people, the high level of noise that comes with busloads of excited children, and overall to help the teachers. I was not prepared to spend the day being responsible for the five boys with the most challenging behaviors in my son's class. It was a day of high anxiety, high sensory issues, being "on" to try to establish a bond with the boys immediately so I had a slight chance they'd listen to me and I could get us all safely through the day.

The teachers left me alone to supervise the boys. I ended up using humor, acting casual, and did get our little group safely through the day: a day that was extremely hot and humid, and filled with high anxiety and major sensory overload. I was constantly watching the boys, going after wanderers, keeping us together, solving problems, managing challenging behaviors, and trying to stay with the rest of their schoolmates as everyone looked at the exhibits. It was beyond exhausting. I was challenged all day with behaviors, sensory assaults, frustration, and trepidation I'd lose a boy(s), and ended the day in a state of high alert, overheated, deflated, with heavily taxed senses, dehydrated, and having failed the expectations of the other teachers, who had worked together and supported each other throughout the day. I just didn't know any of them well enough to get support or know how to join in with them in solidarity to make the field trip great. At least my little group had a good time. It cost me days of exhaustion, withdrawal, and sensory overload.

Challenges in finding supportive networks

The challenge here is to even know what a supportive network is. Most dual diagnosis programs, at least in the USA, seem to focus on substance use disorders paired with mood disorders. If there is little-to-no ASD/PTSD (co-occurring) research, there are even fewer agencies or community health centers—or professional school graduates—able to treat this population.

Another challenge is how the NT world seems to view ASD and PTSD—and disability in general. NTs can talk a good game. But the game is about "helping" the client to fit into our world, "the mainstream." Whether it's ignorance, professional overload, low budget, or lacking cultural competency, helpers would do well to assist clients in those clients' own space (rather than trying to bring them to the mainstream).

Struggles also exist in the masking arena. Many autistic people have language and cognitive skills; yet they mask their autism, cover up social discomfort, and work hard to be someone they are not, so people often see them as "fitting in" just fine. What isn't evident is what's going on inside.

There is a whole realm of chaos going on inside an autistic person masking to fit in.

Lisa writes:

Perhaps the greatest challenge, specifically with support networks, is they consist of people. I'm told that as people we all need connections. I've read we are social beings and need social interactions in order to be well adjusted and happy. It is attempting to build those social connections that can cause chronic traumatic experiences from being rejected over and over again, being ostracized, not accepted, bullied, and not allowed to be with other humans in the same way as non-autistic people; in other words, as we are, rather than as others wish us to be. We are only allowed to build social connections within boundaries put into place by non-autistic people, and those boundaries are not equal. I experience the connections made to usually be superficial, helper to help-ee, obligations, or pity. Nothing lasting. Nothing that stays with me.

I can't put into words the soul-deep feeling of not belonging that comes from being excluded at the very basic level of humanity because the majority of the people in society have deemed you different, burdensome, unworthy, and less-than. Autism is a different neurology from that of non-autistic people. It is considered a social communication disorder because autistic people socialize in ways contrary to how non-autistic people socialize. The integral part of being autistic is being misunderstood and not understanding the neurotypical people of society. Autism is a marginalized subgroup, so it has been left up to us to fit in, despite autistic people being the ones with the social communication disorder.

Behavioral-only therapies

The goal of behavioral therapies such as applied behavioral analysis (ABA) therapy is to extinguish unwanted or harmful behaviors and replace them with "accepted" behaviors. The behaviors to extinguish are determined by parents, teachers, or professionals working with the autistic client, not the client themselves. The means to extinguish the target behaviors are mostly positive and negative reinforcement-based treatment plans. These plans can be traumatic to an autistic client. All behavior is communication, including ABA therapy being implemented by the behavior health professionals. When using ABA therapy to change behaviors unwanted by the people around the autistic client, what is being communicated to the client? Most likely they are learning it's not ok to be themselves, it's not ok to try to communicate in the way they know how, and it's a confusing, traumatic experience. Also, what's happening in many cases is the targeted behaviors are important to the autistic client in areas of self-soothing, communicating, or just being themselves. In essence, they are being systematically, intensely, wholeheartedly trained out of who they inherently are to be someone the people around them might like better. For many autistic people ABA therapy destroys their sense of self.

The smash-up of ASD and PTSD does indeed present the challenge for developing effective therapies and training programs for professionals who work with autistic individuals with PTSD. The first step in doing this is to review the literature on these co-occurring diagnoses. This area is decidedly not well researched. Nevertheless, autistic people with PTSD exist likely in numbers much greater than previously presumed, and they're trying to make their way in the world now. While practitioners are waiting for "best practice" publications, they are treating these patients and clients. Reviewing what is currently known and trying to transfer that learning to a specific case is a good start as we seek to become a part of an effective treatment network.

Chapter V

Research

From childhood to adulthood...

Given that autism is only a relatively recently understood diagnosis, it stands to reason that there are scores of current adults who grew up without proper support. Many of those who were labeled as "geeks" and "weirdos" are now adults, having attained major milestones such as employment, parenthood, homeownership, and other forms of personal independence. These autistic adults with their challenges regarding communication, emotional processing, empathy, loyalty, and other aspects of autism—combined with invisibility and misunderstandings—have been prone to abuse in many traditional forms, as well as via methods the mainstream never thought about until now.

Many would immediately recognize experiences such as sexual assault, natural disaster, accidents, homicide, and war as events that could cause PTSD in the NT population. For autistic individuals, seemingly typical events can cause lasting trauma, too. This adds to the difficulty often encountered in recognizing and diagnosing PTSD and other trauma-related mental health concerns in the ASD population. In addition to different perceptions of trauma, other difficulties include poor assessment tools, and a lack of reporting.

I. Challenges to research
Different perception

One of the major neurological issues in people with an ASD is thought to be the difference in self-awareness and perception of the world around them. The concept of theory of mind states that in order to understand and predict another person's behavior, one must come to understand that others can hold different opinions, goals, motivations, and emotions (Thompson 2017). That skill lends itself to more successful social interactions. In autism, the lack of self-awareness makes it very difficult to understand others, because the autistic person has a flawed reference point. In other words, since the ASD brain typically prevents its owner from imagining another person's motivation, beliefs, and emotions, the autistic person may be unable to partake in meaningful conversation, resolve conflicts, or nurture intimacy.

Also, in terms of perception, as stated earlier, it appears that autistic people may experience severely heightened stress responses to events that a non-autistic person might find benign. Indeed, in a study of Israeli students, researchers found a distinct difference between non-autistic and autistic students regarding destabilizing incidents (Haruvi-Lamdan, Horesh and Golan 2018.) Results indicated that for autistic kids, social experiences such as ostracism are more deleterious to them than are violent events. Other research asserts that "regular" things such as fire alarms, paperwork, pet loss, or off-hand comments can prove overwhelmingly distressful to an autistic person (e.g., Hoover 2015; Kerns, Newschaffer and Berkowitz 2015; King and Desaulnier 2011).

MaryD writes:

A person with ASD, Gus, once imparted to me that as a child he had a traumatic school experience when he overheard an exasperated teacher exclaim that she didn't expect to "be around much longer." Gus became upset and couldn't tell anyone. He couldn't recognize his emotions, and he was unskilled at imagining other meanings for his teacher's statement except what he perceived based on an uncle's recent death. He spent the entire school year running from home to school every day, arriving as teachers drove into the parking lot and staying as late as he could. His guardian was pleased to see such an improved commitment to school. But for Gus, it wasn't schoolwork that motivated him; it was the complete fear that his teacher would die and his entire structure at school would be upended, causing him fear, confusion, and anger. (Note: Gus wasn't focused on his idea that the teacher would die or otherwise leave him—it was that his carefully constructed daily routine would blow up.) He could not imagine what would happen then. He couldn't "problem-solve" or communicate feelings; he could only sleep little, get up early, and run to school each day to make sure his teacher was there when she should have been. He couldn't sleep. His schoolwork suffered. Gus eventually became so overwhelmed with worry that he crashed. It took several weeks for him to get back to functioning state.

So, since many autistic people aren't aware of their inner person, can't naturally imagine a different perception from their own, and might experience traumatic events in a different form than non-autistic people, the problem exists as to how to assess autistics and recognize symptomology relevant to their neurology rather than via the mainstream approach.

Assessment

Indeed, several first-person accounts of how an autistic person experiences trauma are often about things a non-autistic person might never think about. As we've seen, NTs think of extreme events like shootings, sexual assault, and natural disasters to be associated with trauma, but research finds it may be that social incidents, rather than violent ones, are more traumatizing to the autistic person. Thus, many researchers speculate that the *DSM-V* (APA 2013), on which many practitioners and researchers rely for operationalizing diagnoses, is perhaps not sensitive enough to catch PTSD in the autistic population.

What's more, self-report assessment tools are likely invalid for, or at least miss, a lot in the ASD population. One reason for this is that there are no self-assessment tools that are appropriately validated on an ASD population. Thus, clinicians would use tools shown to detect the issue in an NT population. The results aren't helpful, though, because autistic groups and non-autistic groups have very different brain structures, different perceptions of words, different concepts of trauma, and different ways of communicating it. Second, clinicians are asking the autistic client to know about and describe an internal emotional experience, for which the person may have no ability to reference. And last, assessment tools often ask the client to gauge on a scale of, say, 1 through 5, the degree of distress felt in the last week. For an autistic person, this is vague and makes no sense. They may become confused because on Monday ABC happened and they were upset, while on Tuesday XYZ happened in the afternoon, so the morning was good but the afternoon was awful—and it becomes difficult to directly answer a vague question. The overall picture doesn't compute. Plus, they might understand numbers but not the way they're being used and not the intensity, so they spend a lot of time trying to determine what 3 should mean, and then layer that confusion with which day last week? And why not the week before that? And how will it apply to next week? Thus, to determine the type and severity of mental health issues, the practitioner must see each patient as themselves, wholly independent of other patients with ASD or PTSD, in order to discover that person's unique style of communication. Commonly used research tools likely don't capture that.

Underreporting

Again, because an autistic person may not be socially savvy, focusing on details of interest rather than the overall picture, and may be unaware of specific feelings, they often answer only the questions asked of them, in the way they've interpreted them, based on the way the questions were asked. The autism diagnosis may or may not be reported initially, either because the patient doesn't know or because no one asked. Also, the clinician may have an inadequate (read: standard) operational style for autistic clients. Next, the *DSM-V* (APA 2013) may not be sensitive enough to pick up a trauma diagnosis as it relies on objective criteria, whereas the autistic person references only subjective information (Gravitz 2018; Kerns *et al.* 2015). Last, because symptoms overlap between diagnoses, much of the skill of diagnosing lies in the knowledge of differential diagnosis, which doesn't always receive the training and attention it deserves.

Unfortunately, there has been little research into the prevalence of adults with autism and PTSD, let alone how to treat it. Indeed, in her review of emerging research regarding trauma and ASD, Fuld (2018) found that PTSD and other trauma-related disorders are "notably overlooked," and that current constructs of trauma may not be efficient enough for use in the ASD population. In addition, autistic people may not be the best reporters of their symptoms because of communication and emotional experience deficits commonly exhibited in the disorder (Hoover 2015).

The good news is the apparent abundance of research on trauma and stress on children and adolescents/young adults with ASD. Such research is focusing on areas such as initial diagnosing, genetics, brain development, and possible environmental causes.

Regarding research on PTSD in autistic children, as mentioned in Chapter 1, literature reviews reveal that bullying seems to be the main type of trauma investigated, while areas such as anxiety, social isolation, and regression are a considerably smaller focus (Hoover 2015). In calling for an expansion of investigation, many posit the need for greater understanding of how PTSD and other trauma reactions present in autistic kids. For example, because ASD brains typically have trouble with theory of mind and self-awareness, they likely have trouble referencing themselves and so may not be able to connect with the world around them (Thompson 2017). Thus, it has been suggested that considering a trauma patient's subjective experience (personal perspective), rather than focusing on an objective experience (as required by *DSM-V* (APA 2013)) would lessen the chances of members of some groups (such as ASD and intellectual disabilities) being overlooked by medical and mental health clinicians (Kapp 2018). Because some groups of autistic people exhibit heightened stress responses (even to seemingly benign events) and for a longer period of time, it would follow that situations appearing typical and surmountable to NTs may produce much greater stress responses in autistic people. These types of disturbances are unlikely to decrease with age. If this is true, then there is likely a considerable number of autistic people with trauma issues such as PTSD.

The double whammy of ASD and PTSD is that research appears uncertain about how to explore them together. ASD, for example, is heterogeneous in its presentation. This means it manifests itself differently in each person. Despite there being discussion about the co-occurrence of ASD and PTSD, there is little formalized research (Haruvi-Lamdan *et al.* 2018). Operationalizing research constructs is made even more difficult when they smash up together, because symptoms are similar in each and difficult to separate (Gravitz 2018). Still, in reviewing the separate research on each, various researchers posit potential paths seeking to determine associations between the two diagnoses. Those areas include exploring whether ASD increases PTSD symptomology or vice versa, as well as considering whether ASD predisposes one to traumatic experiences, or that ASD people are typically low-resilience (Haruvi-Lamdan *et al.* 2018; King 2010). Finally, in her review of emerging research regarding trauma and ASD, Fuld (2018) found that treatment tends to focus on behavioral, social, and academic needs but that mental health and well-being are rarely studied. This is in the face of a relatively recent review of the quality of life for autistic adults where it was found that autistic people rated quality of life as lower than in the NT group, especially in the areas of social relationships and integration (Ayers *et al.* 2017).

II. Self-advocacy

The Advocacy Alliance helps autistic people by taking action to help them self-advocate for their needs, securing their rights, representing their interests and obtaining services.[1]

Learning about and practicing self-advocacy, particularly for those with autism and PTSD, is important because there is so little research regarding their co-occurrence. Thus, professionals often don't know what to look for or expect. While it is exhausting to continually educate people, it is nonetheless important for the autistic person with PTSD to develop self-advocacy skills. Self-advocacy requires the teacher/patient to understand their own strengths and growth edges so that they can better determine their needs. Once that is organized, the self-advocate

---

1   http://www.theadvocacyalliance.org

can learn how to communicate those needs and accept help with reaching them. This may be a tall order, depending upon the degree of disability; it is, however, imperative to try, because all human rights are important. Advocacy in general promotes equality, inclusion, and justice. Self-advocacy is about empowering yourself to develop choices, make decisions, solve problems, and challenge others to know better. Done effectively, it is not violent or overbearing. Self-advocacy does not use power and control; it seeks to work with others and engage them on your behalf. It requires fair treatment, presumed competence, and openness to understanding from all sides.

In an effort to pursue independence via education and advocacy, people on the spectrum who also have PTSD might be able to help the mainstream by becoming informed of the various research and resources available for each diagnosis independently. For example, according to the World Health Organization (2019), an average of 1 in 160 children worldwide has a diagnosis of autism. The worldwide population suffering from PTSD, perhaps because it can occur resulting from a number of variables coming together, is less centralized. However, reviews of agencies across the globe demonstrate a PTSD rate of 7–8 percent of people in the USA (U.S. Department of Veteran Affairs 2019), roughly 4 percent in England (McManus, Bebbington, Jenkins and Brugha 2014), and 7 percent of people (lifetime rate) in Australia (Australian Bureau of Statistics 2007). In both diagnoses individually, there are many programs and agencies offering support and services. Many of these have an on-line presence.

For example, the Autistic Self Advocacy Network (ASAN) out of the USA offers toolkits that address issues such as budgeting, safety, healthcare, and community-based services.[2] Although the website offers assistance for autism-based issues, many of these

---

2   https://autisticadvocacy.org

issues relate to disability in general and have been quite useful, both directly and for developing ideas for personal self-advocacy. Many of the tools are geared towards the understanding of, and extending towards, inclusive services and events.

ASAN also has an advocacy project based out of Australia and New Zealand, which is part of the larger Australian Autism Alliance.[3] As such, this organization works with public policy to advance opportunities for autistic individuals across Australia. It seeks to bring issues like inclusion and employment to the forefront: "Autistic citizens are capable of contributing to society and enriching the lives of their families and communities.[It is] committed to enable Autistic citizens to achieve their full potential in society" (Autistic Self Advocacy Network).[4]

The National Autistic Society,[5] with physical branches throughout the UK, offers information and explanation on things like history and effectiveness of the UK's Autism Act of 2009 as well as what research is happening and how to go about self-advocating in the UK. It offers education regarding World Autism Awareness Week and how to get involved in that movement. "Advocacy is taking action to help people say what they want, secure their rights, represent their interests and obtain services they need" (Advocacy Alliance).[6]

III. Post-traumatic stress disorder

The US Department of Veterans Affairs' National Center for PTSD offers a plethora of information and trainings for sufferers, friends/family, and professionals.[7] Though the agency is

---

3   www.australianautismalliance.org.au
4   http://a4.org.au/sites/default/files/docs/A4Updates/2008/A4-2008-Update03.pdf
5   www.autism.org.uk
6   https://www.autism.org.uk/about/adult-life/advocacy.aspx
7   www.ptsd.va.gov

primarily focused on trauma regarding military experiences, it offers much to non-military persons as well. This website also contains a self-help section with discussion regarding the development of coping skills and tools. In the research section, the latest "clinically relevant" research is updated fairly frequently. Full text articles are available at no cost.

Similarly, the UK's National Health Service bills itself as the nation's largest on-line health database.[8] It offers information for a myriad of health topics, including access to a national database on various health agencies and hospitals. The website also includes referrals on medications, treatment, social care and support for PTSD sufferers, and the family, friends, and employers of those afflicted. Further, you can use this website to find services by region or specific health topic.

In Australia, Beyond Blue is a website whereby consumers can get specific facts on PTSD and other mental health issues, as well as population-specific assistance.[9] It contains pages of information on symptoms, treatments, and ways to get involved with advocacy. Beyond Blue offers on-line support forums as well as access to national health directories regarding finding mental and medical health professionals.

A better than cursory exploration of the internet reveals scores of autism and PTSD websites where users can learn both general and country-specific information. WARNING: There may be many other websites and organizations that offer help to the autism or PTSD communities. It is important when beginning to use any ideas or services from any assistance or inclusive organization to review things like the board of directors and how the budget uses donations. For example, if there are no directors who identify with the stated mission of the organization, it's likely not the best advocacy to investigate. Also, if an organization raises a lot of

_____

8   www.nhs.uk

9   www.beyondblue.org.au

money but only uses a meagre percentage for actual advocacy, other service agencies might prove more appropriate.

IV. Future directions

As so often happens in research, while some questions are examined, others await. For example, little research exists in terms of gender and how autism and/or PTSD manifest according to gender. While ASD is diagnosed more in males, some suggest that females may be masking more successfully than males (e.g., Hoover 2015). Indeed, conceptualizing the complicated or unfamiliar symptom constellations of ASD/PTSD requires sensitive assessment tools, of which few exist and, of those that do, most were constructed using male subjects. In addition, perhaps because of the lack of attention to context in assessing maladaptive behavior, females may be diagnosed with a personality disorder rather than ASD/PTSD. Gender, assessment, and subsequent treatment present an even greater difficulty for autistic people with PTSD to get help because not only are there few appropriate screening or diagnostic tools, ASD is a syndrome marked by the inability to recognize, describe, or request help when it's needed. The patient can't tell the provider, and the providers haven't recognized it in the client.

Next, quality of life, though important in meaning-making throughout life experience, appears to be neglected in the literature. For example, a recent comprehensive review of evidence-based interventions regarding treatment of children and young adults determined that virtually all reported treatments focused on interventions around behavioral, social, and educational factors (Wong *et al.* 2015). Success in these areas can be measured using qualitative research, wherein responses can be measured rather precisely, tallied, and statistically reported. Such activities might include reducing outbursts, responding in an acceptable manner, and progression to the next grade level. In other words, the study would find out, statistically, whether the autistic person is behaving in a manner expected to be seen, that is, according to what is expected in the mainstream. Quality of life, however, is qualitative and appears to be seldom considered in research. In fact, in more than 400 research articles reviewed, only one focused on mental health and well-being (Wong *et al.* 2015).

Other advocates assert that in the ASD population "the impact of stress and trauma [should be] considered a part of assessment and treatment" (Fuld 2018). Accordingly, in the UK, a recent investigation used an on-line survey to help determine the breakdown between the ASD clients' needs and what the health system is providing (Cam-Crosbie *et al.* 2019). The survey explored specific experiences pertaining to autistic people's perception of treatment and support around the issues of mental illness, self-injury, and suicidality.

In general, the study found a significant number of participants had trouble accessing providers; they noted long waiting lists for treatment, and that support is geared towards autistic children and their caretakers rather than adults. On the occasion that a participant did get treatment, many found that providers often did not have good knowledge of ASD and so often looked to them—the patient—to educate the professional about ASD. Results also indicated a lack of provider understanding regarding autistic individuals with a co-occurring mental health diagnosis. Participants also felt they'd been overlooked, dismissed, or not heard within the health system, with some reporting not receiving help because they appeared to be managing well enough: they had jobs, were students, or were functioning independently. It was noted that perhaps because autistic people manifest emotions differently, they were often misdiagnosed, or that the treatment focused on the wrong goals: in other words, fitting in with the masses rather than learning to recognize emotions (Cam-Crosbie *et al.* 2019).

Immediate research, therefore, might focus on ways to assist autistic people in accessing mental healthcare as well as to help providers recognize ASD and accompanying overloads in general, and specifically in autistic adults who appear to be coping on the outside but may be crumbling on the inside.

Cultural competency

A common focus that all research and opinion pieces reviewed for this section suggests that more emphasis on the importance of practicing (not just knowing about) cultural competency in the ASD world is paramount. ASD is a condition rather than a disorder; the brain sees things differently because it is structured that way. Providers must learn to work within the parameters of that structure, teaching, assisting, and validating the client as they are and according to what would lend quality to their lives, rather than how NTs have been conditioned to expect things.

MaryD provides this simple analogy:

Two life experiences demonstrated to me the need to slow down and think differently from what I had known. The first one was very many years ago when unpracticed adventurers could pay to jump out of airplanes all by themselves, without being attached to an expert. I was one such adventurer. As I was descending after my parachute opened, I found I couldn't reach one of the toggles. That meant I couldn't steer myself. (I was also falling very fast, as I had fudged my weight and been given a smaller chute than I needed!) As I stretched for the toggle, I pushed with my feet, expecting to gain more reach towards the toggle. But, of course, there was no ground beneath my feet—only gravity rushing me towards earth. In the air, there's a different culture, and I had to figure out how to work things differently. I learned to slow my brain in order to think fast.

A second incident—less stressful and also beautiful—was while I was learning to scuba dive. I was taught that when near reefs, if I wanted to see something behind me, I shouldn't turn around head-up as I would on land. I had to bend my body and look through my legs, finding what I was looking for, only from an upside-down view. (When divers just turn around normally, their fins and tanks can greatly harm the reefs, and it might take decades for that nature to recover.)

This has stuck with me: if I wanted to experience what was in the air and sea, I had to adjust my thinking and behavior to those worlds, not to the one I'd become accustomed to on land. When I began to practice in graduate school, I remembered these experiences and gradually learned how to let the situation show me what it needed, rather than trying to fit something into a structured framework. I'm still learning.

Think about it: if one offers a service, shouldn't that person want to serve the patient rather than be served by them? Indeed, the UK study (Cam-Crosbie *et al.* 2019) called for clinicians who are both knowledgeable about ASD and who can be flexible enough to adapt themselves to meeting autistic people where they're at, rather than trying to fit the autistic person into an existing mainstream framework.

Encouragingly, the UK survey also found that the feeling of well-being in autistic clients was significantly increased when participants had experienced support from a provider who was able to understand ASD and who was able to make an individual, relevant plan for treatment and support. Participants in this group also reported a need for a longer term of treatment as making new connections is difficult and takes more time to achieve trust and comfort. When these conditions come together, participants reported feelings of empowerment, autonomy, inclusion, and hope.

Chapter VI

Types of Lived Trauma over Time

Stressful times denote being bombarded with many things at one time, perceived or actual, without sufficient time or ability to address them emotionally, cognitively, spiritually, and/or physically.

(SMAHA 2014)

Trauma complications

In the neurotypical world, there are a multitude of traumatic incidents that can cause PTSD and change neural pathways. Experiences such as interpersonal abuse, bullying, rape, hate-crimes, and natural or man-made disasters leave the potential for a life filled with fear. Research in this area identified personal characteristics of the victims such as perceived intensity of the situation, prior experiences, culture, coping skills, genetics, social support, and several others as potential buffers to processing the fear (e.g., Sayed, Iacoviello and Charney 2015).

For so many on the autism spectrum, however, neurological and environmental differences complicate how someone experiences and processes trauma. Indeed, communication difficulties in general mean they have added challenges in trying to find the right words or other means to communicate what is happening or has happened to them. For example, a slow processing speed complicated by high anxiety is a challenge because ASD people may not be able to keep track of what is happening. In unanticipated or uncertain situations, many ASD people will do or endure what is required of them without knowing quite what is happening or how they feel about it. Only later (sometimes days, weeks or longer) will an autistic person finish processing what happened, and then alexithymia or other feelings-related difficulties can impede seeking help. The confusion can be overwhelming, but subsequent social or behavioral actions aren't necessarily connected to the experiences, so outwardly a victim might be acting as they usually do, but the turbulence inside can be unbearable.

In addition, research demonstrates that autistic people tend to experience various kinds of abuse at rates significantly higher than in neurotypical populations (Weiss and Fardella 2018). This is alarming, particularly given communication difficulties often mean that the process for getting help or otherwise knowing what to do is in itself arduous. Abuse victims with ASD may instead curl up, hands over ears, and try to be invisible. Or they may lash out in meltdown mode, just to make it stop—and be chastened for aggression rather than being recognized as overwhelmed and hurt. Finally, and perhaps most importantly, is the element of profundity. In autism, things that NTs might take in their stride, like grazing a guard rail (almost driving off the road), can give an autistic person higher-than-NT anxiety and fear as they search to make sense of what happened and why. This strife is likely to be invisible or even dismissed by the NT community because it may seem like the event is "no big deal." More isolation, less support, and fewer coping resources make autistic people at considerably higher risk for developing PTSD. The following are situations that can cause and/or trigger PTSD in autistic adults. While there will be some "normal" traumatic experiences, there will also be what could be deemed benign experiences to non-autistic people.

I. Rejected, ostracized, invisible

It is sometimes said that because autistic people don't understand social nuances, being left out of things doesn't bother them. That would be useful, if it were true. Instead, it is a very harmful myth. Autistic people desire belongingness, too, and they suffer without it. Inclusion is an important element in healthy relationships. Whether animal or human, being shunned or put out of the group is generally unsafe; it leaves the non-member without protection and more vulnerable to predators. When included in a group, the person is able to learn from other members; they develop and hone talents, as well as learn about themselves in relation to others. The group as a whole benefits from various individual skills, learning social techniques, problem-solving, and other proficiencies important to survival. Isolation, on the other hand, impedes growth and causes pain, both mental and physical. It can change brain function and stymie social, professional, and romantic development.

Below, Lisa shares some experiences that have caused her extreme pain and confusion as a result of rejection, ostracism, or invisibility:

Blame the label

Lisa shares:

> I follow social etiquette, try hard to make no social blunders, and apologize for any I do make—only to experience some non-autistic people who don't use social etiquette, are rude, bully, patronize, or ignore me, then blame botched social interactions on me simply because of my diagnosis of autism. It seems to be socially acceptable to blame me because I'm autistic and then stop there, instead of looking at themselves and trying to do better.

Literalness

In learning and expressing themselves through language, non-autistic people seem to use language more often according to its implied meaning. For autistic people, however, words are mostly understood via their literal meaning. This in itself can cause many misunderstandings and breakdowns in communication leading to rejection or ostracism. Autistic people can get lost in conversations when the true meanings of words are arbitrarily changed, where even something as simple as, "text ya later!" meaning, "see ya later!" can feel awfully lonely when no text comes later on. Then come the hours of figuring out what could've possibly gone wrong, when nothing was ever wrong at all.

Another way of talking where words do not mean what they say is with metaphors. Consider these examples: "He has a chip on his shoulder" (I don't see it); "She fell for that hook, line and sinker" (is she ok, did that hurt her?); "It's a piece of cake" (where's the cake?); and "Laughter is the best medicine" (what's the second best?). Although these statements can be funny to an autistic person once they've learned them, if a social situation has become confusing, misunderstandings can happen pretty quickly. The rejection and ostracism come when an autistic person can't keep up with the conversation, can no longer participate, and is ultimately left out.

Then, there are times when non-autistic people will say something alarming that can be perceived as concrete truth, when it was actually just words strung together with no real meaning at all. The trauma comes from the possibility of what was said actually being true, as well as the reaction of non-autistic people when autistic people do not understand their confusion. What typically happens next is that preconceived notions about autistic people, such as being socially awkward, less-than, and different, are validated, and any possible combination of rejection, bullying, anger, or ridicule may be expressed towards the autistic person.

An example of this was shared by an autistic adult, as follows:

> Certain memories stay with me for decades. One Christmas morning, my father told me that I should "enjoy this Christmas" because he "wouldn't be here next year." I was horrified. I managed to get through the morning feigning happiness, but my insides were desolate. As his statement settled in my mind, I began to feel like I couldn't leave the house or something bad would happen. For months I stayed home whenever I could or, if I had no choice of going somewhere, I was always in a hurry to get back home. I was afraid he would leave, and I needed to be there when he did so I could stop him. My fear—my intense focus for those months—was from him basically telling me that he was deserting me. I was teased by my family for staying in the house all the time. I was taunted for not having friends. My fear was misunderstood as laziness. I found out much later that he was just angry for getting tools for Christmas...again...like he did every year. He only said those words "wouldn't be here next year" because he was angry. He didn't mean them literally. Yet, it cost me months of fear. Words having different meanings than what was directly said had no significance in my life. I took the words literally and it caused a lot of anxiety, confusion, and misunderstandings for me.

II. Loss of relationships over time

The process of making, developing, and maintaining friendships can be harrowing or even traumatic for autistic people. Many have had adverse experiences of rejection, misunderstandings, and friendships that just fade away for no apparent reason.

For people who have endured one failed friendship after another for years, a new friendship does not only include the new person, it includes all the other people who have rejected them as friends, used them for their skills, or promised things not delivered. The potential for every negative friendship scenario an autistic person has endured is possible in that one new friend. It can feel like a tremendous risk to trust.

Relationships take a long time to build for an autistic person. The social communication of making, keeping, and maintaining relationships is one of the more difficult aspects of being autistic. Of course, there are autistic people who honestly do not want or need relationships. They are fine being alone pursuing their passions and enjoying life as they please; but there are far more who do want relationships yet have great difficulty in the area of social interactions.

Lisa shares:

> What I have experienced throughout my adult life is friendships are difficult to make, harder to develop, and confusing to maintain. One reason friendships are difficult to make is that most of them start with small talk. I avoid small talk if I can. It does not make sense to talk about shallow, arbitrary, daily "things." I get bored, and my mind wanders.
>
> The friendships I've found, who accept me for who I am, have lasted for 20+ years. Those are not just local friends I see regularly; they are also on again/off again friendships where we just continue on from where we left off no matter how much time has gone by since we saw each other last. I trust and cherish these friendships.
>
> I also have many friendships that just disappear and I have no idea why. The other person will suddenly not return phone calls, texts, or even letters in the mail. There is no more friendship. I'm left wondering if one ever even existed, although I have proof through pictures and memories.

I do have some theories. One theory is my friend just got tired of being in a friendship with me. That's where my brain goes, straight to negative interpretations due to PTSD. I feel that being friends with me must be burdensome, maybe because they have to clarify themselves for me, or they don't understand I can't always join them when they invite me places because I'm overwhelmed, or I'm just too different. What happens when I meet someone is that I have a mask on so I can appear to be what's "normal" to them and fit in. This is the person they become friends with and get to know over a period of time. As I relax into the relationship, however, the mask comes off slowly and carefully, showing who I really am: I believe my missing friend didn't like me with my mask off.

Why I say that is because once the mask begins to slip, what typically happens next is small changes, such as shortened visits, fewer visits, emotional distance, and awkwardness. I will ask them if everything is ok and, what I have found is they will answer back that nothing is wrong. Yet, something is wrong. I know it. I'm so in tune to changes, I detect subtle ones. I am so sure something is wrong, I will ask again, either then or the next time we are together. I feel an anxiety-riddled impending doom. Frequently what happens is my friend continues to tell me nothing is wrong, and not to worry. The next thing I know, I don't hear from them anymore. I might call, text, or email, but there is no answer. They are gone from my life. Just gone. If I ever do see them again, and have a chance to ask what went wrong, they won't tell me things like the friendship became too difficult, they were exhausted, or my differences became too much for them. They might say they got really busy with life. It seems if that was the reason, they could've simply let me know. I have no way to learn to do friendships any other way; therefore, it happens again, and again, and again with other friendships. It happens so often that trust becomes a definite issue and then, like I said earlier, I start being unsure of a friendship from the start, which makes that friendship last an even shorter period of time.

Accepting compliments

Unfortunately, many autistic adults who were bullied, hurt, and abused in their youth tend to have a hard time with positive things like compliments. I can't handle compliments. They give me physical pain sometimes. I dread them. I don't know what to say because the person giving the compliments is being nice, yet it hurts to hear them. They don't know they are hurting me, so I also feel very disconnected from them. It is a hurtful, lonely experience for me to hear compliments. It's a quandary as well in that the people who can hurt me the most with compliments are the people I'm closest to because of them knowing me well enough to give straight-to-the-heart gut-wrenching compliments. I feel they should know that I really don't deserve the plaudits. I do not want to hurt anyone's feelings, so if someone I know and trust gives me compliments, I try to accept them, and if I can't, I say, "I'm not accepting compliments today." The reason I say that is because some days are harder to accept compliments than others.

All that said, compliments are also, hopefully an objective way of measuring how I'm doing and how someone feels about me. They are useful, nice, but just hurt too much.

III. Everyday struggles

Lisa describes how her everyday struggle feels:

I feel like I'm walking through a dark, creepy room where at every movement a giant, loud Jack-in-the-box jumps up and starts playing eerie music that everyone else already knows what to do about, but makes no sense to me. The room

> has just enough light in it to see that the spider webs in the
> corners are empty because the spiders are out on the prowl
> looking for me. The feeling this description evokes as it is
> being read is a feeling I have, but can't name.

Living with ASD/PTSD means spending most days with fear,
hypervigilance, anxiety, and flashbacks, as well as all that is
autism, such as communication issues, sensory reactivity, and
the need for uniformity.

There's also an extra sensitive vulnerability in always having
to explain yourself to people, especially if you're not sure of
the situation you're trying to fit into. As with friendships, an
autistic person with PTSD often finds it necessary to divulge the
diagnosis to other people in the course of a day or experience
negative feedback of being different. Even people who should
know about diverse populations (like SpecEd instructors or
hospital staff) can react to the person with ASD/PTSD before
them as they "expect" to see them. For example, autistic people
with PTSD tend to be extra quiet, or quite direct (i.e. without
flowery words or typical niceties, which aren't a part of their
comfort level) and their communications can appear as if they
are rude or trying to be difficult. Then, to add to a painfully
misinterpreted interaction, the NT person can react "in kind,"
meaning they often are difficult right back at them! This creates
huge misunderstandings—and the autistic person with PTSD
is inclined to retreat or rebel, adding to the confusion and
frustration, often resulting in more trust issues. If the problem
absolutely requires a solution, such as a school issue for their
child, the autistic person with PTSD has to persevere—despite
a lack of confidence or energy. Thus, they have to inform the
admin of their diagnosis and then all of sudden, things change,
which can be good, for this particular situation perhaps.
But then every problem seems to be blamed on the label,
there's a chance they are pitied, and taking the time to find out

how to communicate with the person isn't considered anymore, because they are autistic. Many times the diagnosis serves to be the source of any and all communication difficulties before the disclosure and every one from then on afterwards.

Even more unfortunate is that autistic people with PTSD have to pair these struggles with a pervasive sense of physical and mental insecurity; they are hypervigilant, always on the alert for someone who isn't telling the truth or has hidden expectations of them. They may have to try to discern if what they are hearing is actually what someone truly meant, and if the information they give will be used against them later—in terms of embarrassment, rejection, or being patronized. It can boil down to two things: the NT people often see what they expect to see from an autistic person (which isn't always what's actually before them), and the autistic person with PTSD has to be self-protective in any way that feels most safe, regardless of the helping person's motivations. It's exhausting.

IV. Changes in routine

Change is an unexpected deviation from routine. Lots of things change during a day, and this brings major challenges. One aspect of autism is the compulsion to adhere to routine and avoid change. Autistic people can find safety and comfort in having a daily routine. PTSD people do, too. For the autistic person with PTSD, there is so much sensory stimulation to absorb, relationship difficulties to smooth over, social situations to manage, thoughts to process, and safety to find that having a routine to simply follow helps immensely to have a successful day. Changes to that routine disrupt the balance of life autistic adults are trying so diligently to persevere with. In coping with change, many times an autistic person with PTSD can be triggered.

For autistic people, changes are not just frustrating, they can be devastating. Experiencing a change in routine can be traumatic depending on what has changed. Change leaves an autistic person unbalanced, unnerved, confused, vulnerable, and highly anxious. Change is upsetting because the safety net that was carefully constructed through preplanning for any conceivable mishap is suddenly gone. Change has wiped out all the preparations, back-up plans, and alternative arrangements, leaving discord and confusion.

Lisa explains:

> I try my best to prevent any possible changes I might encounter during the day. I may double-check appointment times, verify meeting places, check to see if who I'm meeting is still coming, or even ask people to let me know ahead of time if there's a change in plans. The reason I go to all this trouble is to avoid experiencing unexpected change.

Hence, transition can be a distressing change for autistic people. There are many types of transitions that happen during life such as: starting a new job or school, adding a new family member, or even holidays when routines change temporarily with travel, visiting, and parties. This type of change can be prepared for so the experience can be more successful, yet it is still quite difficult.

With change being a part of life, autistic people encounter changes regularly. Masking can help to alleviate an embarrassing reaction to change, but only for a while. The energy it takes to mask during a change experience is tremendous, leaving the autistic person with very little stamina left to persevere through the rest of the day. Certainly, after a day with several unexpected changes in it, an autistic person may need to get home where it is safe, sensory friendly, quiet, and dimly lit so they can pursue self-care. However, PTSD complicates this safe place because it's inescapable. Even after leaving an overwhelming environment, PTSD can potentially add flashbacks, a negative outlook, intrusive thoughts, and anxiety above and beyond what autism itself produces, so the safety of home is not dependable.

Emergency situations

Emergency situations are exponentially difficult unplanned changes to routine. On top of being unanticipated and so difficult to manage, emergencies can either trigger or cause PTSD. There's a shock involved due to the senses being assaulted from many different directions, at a high intensity, and all at once. For an autistic person with PTSD, a typical emergency situation consists of three parts. The first is when it happens. Whatever the emergency is, it has begun. Something drastic just happened. The world just changed. There needs to be a reaction, quickly! Working with varying processing speeds, social challenges, a sensory explosion, triggers, anxiety, and so much more—a reaction needs to be made quickly and efficiently whether an autistic person with PTSD is helping themselves or someone else. The second part is when all the help arrives. There are sirens, lights, crowds of people, odours, screaming, and officials demanding explanations so they can assess the emergency and start helping. The third part of an emergency is afterwards. There is so much to process. There could be a flood of leftover emotions to sort through, or a deep, solid, impenetrable numbness to experience.

Lisa shares:

> I caused a car accident once. I had just dropped my son off at school for the day and was heading home with my toddler. I was distracted by something and when I looked up there was a car stopped right in front of me. I was going about 20 mph. I slammed on my brakes and then slammed into the car. I heard nothing at the time, as if reality were suspended.
> Then, my whole world exploded.

We hit...I felt every sense my body can feel...like a punch in the face. I instantly felt like the worst person ever. I felt like my life changed forever because I caused someone else pain. I felt powerless to fix something that was unfixable. I couldn't consciously decide anything. I couldn't think except to be on autopilot.

I was dazed as I assessed the situation. The impact of the airbag was violent. The smell was of repugnant chemicals. I quickly checked myself for injuries. I then checked my son. He was also dazed, but seemed ok at first glance. Next, I headed for the occupants of the vehicle I rear-ended. I was so scared. Fear of looking in and seeing them unconscious, or worse. Fear there was a child not strapped in a car seat correctly. Fear of seeing injuries I caused. Fear of everything that could possibly be horrible...because of me. In that moment I would've given anything to turn back time and make a different choice. The front door of the car was maybe a 10-foot walk from my car, but seemed to take forever. There was an older gentleman inside. He was belted. His airbag did not deploy on him and he was talking. I asked him if he was ok. He said yes.

Then, a second explosion of my world.

Suddenly, I could hear everything! There was a cacophony of fire trucks, police cars, first responders, people watching, talking, lights, smells, the terrible scene itself, and questions to answer. I tried to ignore all the sensory stimuli as I walked up to the first police officer I saw, told them everything I did. We talked further and he told me where to stand. I didn't leave that spot for the next hour or so; I was afraid of leaving that spot. I was planted there. I can remember just wanting the man in the car to get help and be ok. My mind was hyperfocused. I felt like my brain was an eight-lane highway, merging into one. I had no words. I couldn't think, and I was thinking of everything. Finally, I got a ticket and stern words from the police officer. Then, I dared to leave my spot.

At home, I was able to wash away the chemicals from the airbag, but the emotions I started to feel weren't going anywhere. They came in waves crashing into my heart. I had hurt someone. I had caused an accident. I felt like I was never going to be ok again. I couldn't make my mind rest, and I was exhausted with worry and self-damnation. For the rest of that day, I cried and slept and cried some more. Aches and pains came and I felt like I got run over by a truck. To this day, the feeling post-crash stays with me...that immediate feeling of hurting someone, dread.

V. Overwhelming sensory input

Sensory overload can develop when more than one sense is receiving information from the environment all at once. There is a lot of processing to be done to regulate from sensory overload. Moreover, for people living with ASD/PTSD, sensory input can trigger flashbacks. Flashbacks bring people back to a traumatic memory complete with its own set of sensory stimulation. A simple trip to the store can turn into an anxiety-filled, fearful, overwhelming experience if triggered by sensory input from the environment. Perhaps someone sees a person or place very similar to where a traumatic event took place. There could be a smell that reminds them of a trauma they endured, an unexpected touch, or they hear a song, shout, or voice that brings them to a place of reliving a traumatic event. It feels like it is actually happening, not something that has happened...*is* happening. An autistic person runs the risk of being triggered by sensory input wherever they go.

In the picture below, the smash-up between autism, PTSD, and sensory overload is shown. While PTSD causes the fear, anxiety, flashbacks, and negative outlook for an autistic person, causing them to withdraw and close down, it is the sensory overload that keeps them from being able to reach out and get the help they need. It's sensory overload that causes them to be stuck and unable to move. Managing the three challenges together is truly a difficult task.

Fortunately for some, there may be ways to alleviate the challenges of overwhelming sensory input. For example, one can be proactive and leave a place before the sensory input becomes overwhelming. Having a pre-established time limit can help with leaving at an opportune time. Another way is to choose places to go that are sensory friendly. There are more and more places having sensory friendly rooms or special sensory friendly days for people with sensory issues. Choosing the right time to go can help reduce sensory stimulation. Rainy (showery) days can be the best time to go to an amusement park. Many places have graphs showing high-volume traffic days to make it easier to pick the best day to visit. Planning to go to an event early or arrive late can help with sensory overload. And, finally, resting before an event can help an autistic person enjoy an event and even stay longer. The idea is to rest in an environment that is quiet, soothing, and calm, with the right kind of music, temperature, noise level, and decor. Each autistic individual with PTSD has to find out for themselves what works. Each NT person might try to help them manage their needs as appropriate.

Autistic burnout

Autistic adults are susceptible to high levels of unhealthy stress (Mills 2016). Because of the range of symptoms, other possible diagnoses, and difficulty identifying emotions, autistic adults may not recognize the cause of their discomfort as stress right away. There's only a certain amount of stress any one person can take before they are no longer able to cope and have to change something in their life for the better or there are consequences. They may keep going beyond their limit and sink into what is known in the autism community as an "autistic burnout."

The leading cause of autistic burnout is camouflaging, a coping skill that is utterly exhausting to maintain. A study showed, "[c]amouflaging was frequently described as being mentally, physically, and emotionally draining; requiring intensive concentration, self-control, and management of discomfort" (Hull *et al.* 2017). Masking also leaves an autistic person with a soul-deep sense of not belonging to the world they live in due to knowing why masking is necessary. The knowledge of having to essentially erase who you are as a person to be accepted as a member of society is deeply harmful to the psyche; so much so, the consequences can be inescapable: "Although compensating for their difficulties may help people with ASD connect with others, get jobs, and successfully navigate social situations, accumulating research suggests it can also lead to exhaustion, burnout, anxiety, and depression." (Hull *et al.* 2017).

Autistic burnout permeates every area of life. Skills in areas such as executive functioning, social communication, self-care, managing emotions, and masking can regress until an overall appearance of being more autistic is reached. Physical and/or psychological symptoms can manifest in areas such as speaking, memory loss, emotions, and/or digestive issues and illness in general. Speaking can be affected in either the lack of ability to express what the individual needs or selective mutism. Additionally, emotions may be too volatile to manage coping skills, and meltdowns may come more frequently.

There are ways to manage and alleviate autistic burnout. One is to remember to take time or self-care. The best type of self-care is individualized to each person. Whatever helps the most to calm down, relax, and help the negative thoughts to dissipate is beneficial. Another way to avoid autistic burnout is to be prepared for any negative social situations, to make strong boundaries, and leave if and when feelings of being overwhelmed are experienced. Autistic burnout can last for days, weeks, months, or be permanent. Since camouflaging is the leading cause of autistic burnout, perhaps one more way autistic adults can help themselves is to be themselves.

VI. Suicidal ideation and other self-harm

Lisa shares how emotional pain can lead to suicidal thoughts:

I understand now how people can come to have suicidal thoughts. The despair and emotional pain is so deep, so consuming, gut-wrenching, tiring and goes on for so long; it's a comfort to think of it ending. In the moment, there is no thought of family, friends, or hurting anyone else. In the moment, there is no thought of what you might miss out on, that life is precious, or things might change. There is only the deep, dark, all-consuming pain that you need to relieve, to get away from, and to escape. Pain from emotions that hurt so much it becomes a physical pain with no physical connection to relieve it. Emotions so enormous they feel like a roaring, churning tornado inside the worst hurricane imaginable wiping everything good away.

Suicidality in autism, both in ideation and action, as well as other self-harming behaviors are grossly understudied. Some research suggests that it occurs primarily in ASD populations with a co-occurring disorder such as anxiety or depression, and in higher functioning autistic people (e.g., Bennett 2016). Thus, the question often reviewed is whether the problem is associated with the ASD symptoms or the co-occurring mental health conditions. Some suggest that trouble in the ASD domains of communication, cognition, and social support may lead to increased vulnerability for self-harming, while others propose that the mental health component is the primary motivator. A recent case study out of France sought to sort out this question. Researchers were able to determine that parts of ASD, such as the repetitive thinking, rigidity, and compulsive thinking patterns—aspects unique to ASD rather than anxiety or depression—appear to be linked to suicidal/self-harm thinking (e.g., Weiner *et al.* 2019). Indeed, being unable to recognize emotions, communicate them well, or ask for help, as well as having thinking processes that can produce repetitive thinking about how to escape pain, loneliness, sadness, and fear seem like they would be an extraordinary recipe for self-harm and suicidal behaviors.

Lisa writes:

I believe suicide ideation is within the minds of many people diagnosed with autism, and especially if they have PTSD as well. It's not an inherent characteristic of autism; it's a result of living in an NT world with a diagnosis of autism. It's not belonging. It's being misunderstood at the deep level of self. Understanding the truth in having to become someone you're not in order to be accepted by society in general can develop into an intense rejection of who you are, which can result in suicide ideation. There is an unfathomable grief in not only having to live in an environment not made for you, but to also feel like your peer's main goal is to change you into something you are not to make themselves more comfortable. It leaves an autistic person feeling unwanted, less-than, rejected, and alone.

Think about this for a second—you live in an alien environment in which you must have time to recharge and manage self-care just to continue to live in it. The other people living in the environment reject, misunderstand, and do not accept you, and for the most part you are alone. When you are with people, they try to change you to be more like them. You relent and lose yourself in order to be at least accepted superficially by the people in the alien environment. You work exhaustingly hard to be someone you are not to fit in, but it's difficult to sustain because it's so draining to mask who you are so completely in the presence of others. So, your time with people is limited enough that it doesn't cover the essential need to be connected with others. Moreover, when you are alone and can be yourself again, you know deep down inside that nobody in your world knows you as yourself. That is enough to bring on thoughts of suicide ideation.

Reaching out for help is difficult for autistic people because it is a social skill and does not come naturally. The weak connections to society and negative social interactions also cause a lack of trust in autistic people. If someone does reach out, it's important to know how to be there for them in a way they can understand.

How to help

When struggling to help someone with ASD/PTSD, there are things that help, and things—some of which seem perfectly appropriate to say—that do not help (and can actually harm the person). When the helper's attention is fully on the person before them, remembering and using the below suggestions can change everything for the person in need.

The following is from a feature story from *Spectrum Women* magazine (Morgan 2018b):

Here are five suggestions on what *not* to say:

- *Everything will be ok.* No, it's not ok, nothing is ok. In the moment this feels dismissive and condescending.

- *You have so much to be thankful for*...which may be true, but the suicide ideation remains. It doesn't go away because there are things to be thankful for any more than a person with a fatal disease can make *it* go away by being thankful for what *they have.* For me, suicide ideation is not a feeling or a personal fault. It's an intrusive thought process of the brain.

- *You just need to think about good things.* That is not going to help. It's like telling a person who is paralyzed that if they think enough about good things, they will be able to get up and walk.

- *Have you told anyone?* Yes! They are telling you! A person reaching out for help is not a conversation; it's a call to action.

- *There's nothing I can do for you.* Don't say that. Just don't. They haven't called to ask you to "do" anything.

Hearing there's nothing that can be done is defeating and hopeless. They most likely don't want to be alone with their thoughts anymore and are looking for a connection.

And, here are five suggestions for what to say to a person struggling with suicide ideation:

- *I'm glad you called.* After reaching out, it feels comforting to know it was ok to call.

- *You matter.* With all the negative thoughts swirling around in the mind of someone with suicide ideation, hearing that they matter can make a huge difference in the way they view themselves in the moment.

- *I love and care about you.* Oh! A connection to another person has just been made. Telling someone they are loved and cared for is one of the best things to say.

- *What do you need?* This is such a sweet question. It's a reminder to the person reaching out that they are being thought of as a person who is still strong enough to share what they need in the moment, instead of being thought of as a weak person, incapable of thinking for themselves because their brain is being uncooperative with thoughts of suicide.

- *You can call/text again if needed.* This statement leaves the door open for a person with suicide ideation to know they are not alone and can reach out again if the struggle gets too difficult.

Chapter VII

Exploitative Relationships

bullying...happens between two people with different influence... Bullies hurt by repeatedly teasing, gossiping, or otherwise attacking you. It's a form of social power; they act badly in order to make you feel less than them so they can gain (or keep) their status above you.

(Donahue 2018, p.9)

Vulnerability in autism

Autistic people of any age are vulnerable to bullies and other exploitation. According to the US Department of Education (2016), more than one in five children are bullied in the USA, with autistic children bullied at a substantially higher rate. Other forms of exploitation occur in the areas of finances, sexual harassment, trafficking, use of personal property, and social grooming. Exploitation means that someone is treating another dishonorably and benefiting from it. Targets typically experience results that are very painful and often life changing, but not in a helpful way.

Autistic people are at an increased danger from exploitation for several reasons. First, this is because autistic people are generally honest and upfront about their thoughts, and they expect that others are, too. They typically expect that what they see is the truth. The autistic mind typically can't conceive of any different way. Second, autistic people are naturally very cooperative. It doesn't occur to them that they have a choice about doing or not doing something another person asks of them. They also tend to be concerned with being polite, and saying "no" is viewed as disrespectful. Finally, many autistic people desire inclusion and approval. If someone creates that expectation for them, the autistic person is often very willing to comply. Their good nature makes them ripe for predators. Below are some experiences relating to the more common, and very harmful, forms of exploitation and abuse.

I. Bullying in childhood

Lisa writes:

> I was in first grade. A boy named Joey was next to the window looking outside. It was cloudy and the sky was dark. He said, "It's going to rain." I remember thinking that I had something I could actually say that might not sound stupid to my peers! I stepped near him and said, "It's too cold to rain, it's going to snow." Joey turned around and announced to the kids near us that I said it was too cold to rain! Then he started chanting, "Duh! Duh! Duh! It's too cold to rain," with a funny look on his face. The other students started chanting it too. I don't remember a teacher getting involved. A lot of times the bullying by a bunch of kids happened while the teacher stepped out for a moment. I heard that chant for a long time after that day. The students deemed me stupid. What I did not understand was, even after it snowed instead of raining, they didn't stop making fun of me. Also, why was what I said so bad? Didn't they know there was a certain temperature where it would snow instead of rain? If they were all making fun of

me for just knowing the truth, was it really being made fun of, or was it something else? This incident, and many more like it, confirmed that I was different; that I didn't fit in. They created and contributed to a lifelong intense feeling of loneliness.

I was the bullied one in my classroom, which was organized alphabetically by our last names, and we all stayed together as a class until we graduated high school. Throughout grade school, I never was able to break out of my role of the "kid who was bullied." The best thing that happened was once we hit high school, I was ignored and learned I was invisible.

As a teen, I was bullied by a neighborhood boy who was bigger than I was and oh, how he hated me, and he let me know it. He constantly called me names, humiliated me, and generally terrorized me whenever he could...mostly out of sight. He was smart about that. I tried to avoid him. One day, a few houses away from mine and right in front of his, he tried to punch me. I had some defensive moves—a necessity—and was able to block his punch. This only proved to enrage him. So, he came at me again, and as we went back and forth—me trying to get away mostly, him trying to hurt me mostly—he elbowed me hard in the stomach. I was doubled over, waiting for the next blow to land, when I heard him laughing before he disappeared into his house. I made my way home, didn't tell anyone at home, didn't tell anyone anywhere, and went on with life, now more fearful of my neighborhood. I felt so defeated, like I was unable to affect my own life. I couldn't fight, I couldn't get away. I couldn't tell anyone. I couldn't process anything except that I failed. I spent a lot of time trying to figure out why he hated me, why anyone did the things to me that they did. I tried to be better, but I didn't understand how.

MaryD reports:

I recently had cause to be observing a playground during an after-school program for elementary kids. I saw two boys talking to each other, one rather animatedly. He appeared joyful while the other showed a blunted affect and looked confused. The animated kid was trying to get the other one to dance to a song; it was obvious that he didn't want to, but he did anyway. It seemed fishy to me, so I asked the aide what was up. It seemed that the dancing child, Jay, is autistic. He is sweet, focused, and likes to do a good job. The other kid, Robbie, had found out that Jay listens to a specific song and dances in a room before the school bell (as a means of calmly entering his day). For the last few days, he'd been gathering people around to watch Jay do his dance and they laughed hysterically. The teachers watched, too. Engaging the adults in conversation revealed that none had thought this might be an exploitative experience for Jay. One teacher told me that she'd asked Jay if he wanted to do the dance and he said he did. Further probing, however, revealed that she'd asked him a yes-or-no question where the obvious answer would be cooperative, that she'd asked it in front of Robbie and his friends, the people Jay wanted to please, and that Robbie had been in Jay's space yelling, "yes yes yes" the whole time. Later, when his aide addressed Jay again in private about the song and dance, Jay stated that he only liked to do the dance before his class "where it's special" but that he didn't want to hurt his friends' feelings. He also noted he didn't like to dance on the playground because it made his belly hurt.

People who are not versed in autism would think that Jay was doing what he wanted to do. In the world of autism, however, he was not given a choice. He was asked a closed question in front of others, where he could only answer "yes." The kids were allowed to laugh and point. Jay's dance was exploited for entertainment instead of protected as a regulating tool. And even though he didn't say he felt bad, his belly told the story. That playground experience was unsafe for him.

II. Bullying in adulthood

Lisa states:

As an adult, the bullying is stealthier and harder to realize. Just like life is not as simple as it was in grade school, bullying is not as simple as it was back then either. As life goes on, there are more intricate layers of social understanding and convoluted relationships to figure out. One example of this was back in 2007...

I went to a routine meeting at a church where I met four other ladies to pray. It was the birthday of one of the ladies and I had brought her a plant. When I entered the room, I could immediately tell the ladies were stiff and uncomfortable. I gave the plant to the birthday girl and sat down. Instead of friendly greetings, I got mean stares and harsh questions. I did not know what any of them was talking about. I was being asked over and over again why I lied. When I asked what they were talking about, I was told that I already knew what they were talking about and to not act like I didn't. I had no idea. I went into fight-or-flight mode and got up to leave. The two ladies on either side of me held my arms down to the table and wouldn't let me up. They wanted answers to questions I couldn't give them. I still do not know what happened or what they were asking me about. The next week another meeting was called that I "had" to attend. I was extremely apprehensive, and rightly so because I didn't learn much more about what they thought I did. I had a three-month gag order put on me by them. I could not talk to anyone in the church for three months! I could only talk to them, and only if I asked first and they said yes. I left that church. This was a bullying situation I didn't see coming. I had the mindset of finding out what I did so I could fix it. The ladies were the only "friends" I had, yet I gave it up for a sense of peace and fairness to me.

In general, bullies using me as their physical targets or verbal punching bag, and my inability to communicate that, process it with someone safe, and figure out the meaning has cast a wide net of negativity over most subsequent social interactions. In being exploited for what others perceive as a weakness, I am irrevocably changed. It confirms and reconfirms what I've known all along: I'm different, less-than, and I don't belong with people. On my bad days, I am certain that I cause problems just by being alive and breathing. If I looked deep down inside of myself, there would be this ugly, shriveled up, less-than person who doesn't deserve to matter to anyone. The bullies can see that right away. They don't have to look deep down inside, they just know it. It's like they can sense it, and that gives them permission to bully me.

It helps me to know I'm not the only one who feels that way about me. It shows me I'm not wrong in how I feel about myself. None of those ladies in the story above ever showed any remorse for what they did. They felt justified. I believed that if four people all felt the same way, it must be true. It can't be that they were wrong and one person (me) was right. I knew they were right because I got a certified letter in the mail kicking me out of the church by all four of them, the associate pastor, and several deaconesses. How else could anyone ever look at that, except as truth?

Here's where the PTSD comes in: People can tell me all they want that I'm a good, successful person who matters, but I know differently. I know what the bullies know. The bullies are not big mean kids in grade school, they are honest people—pastors, neighbors, family, friends, therapists, bosses, and doctors. They are upstanding members of society; the problem is, they don't see me as a member of their society, so they feel no connection to me, nor I to them, and bullying becomes validated as survival of the fittest in this ruthless world. That's how I see things. It's safer to expect what I know. Any further risk will only produce more hurt.

III. Gaslighting

This is a form of control that many people use to confuse others and overwrite their reality. While mostly used as a control tactic, it can also be done unconsciously. For example, when a child sees or hears his parents get hurt—things crashing, yelling, crying—the child becomes afraid and seeks reassurance. His parent, caretaker, protector tells him everything is alright. The child knows it's not, but he's trained to look to his caretaker (i.e., social referencing) to interpret for him. He saw it or heard it—he knows that. Since he can't doubt "the big people" (i.e., authority), he comes to doubt himself. The more truths are denied, the more confused he gets. Over time, he learns not to trust himself or his perception.

Gaslighting in romantic or socially important adult relationships is a fundamentally heinous tactic; a psychological type of abuse that happens slowly, over time, with lies, manipulation, set-ups, and the perpetrator stubbornly denying the truth, even in the face of clear proof. And their rationale seems so logical. The victim is worn down over time with the lies, half-truths, insults, and even positive reinforcement to confuse them further. The most confusing situation is when the abuser lets the relationship go smoothly, making the victim feel closer, share thoughts and dreams, make memories...and then a very small mistake is made by the victim (or no mistake at all), and everything falls apart. Again. The abuser grows cold, stops talking (rejects his victim), plays the victim role, and blames everything that fell apart on his prey. It's a miserable time for victims because it's clear that it was their fault; they might be accused of not wanting the relationship enough, of not loving enough, of being a bad person, and many other accusations that whittle self-esteem down to nothing. What was right is now wrong—so what's right? Because that feels wrong, too.

Try this—nod your head and say to yourself "No" with each nod. Then shake your head from side to side and say "Yes" each time. Nod, "No." Shake, "Yes." See how uncomfortable that is to go against what you know to be true? (Truth = Nod "Yes." Shake "No.") That's what gaslighting feels like. The victim knows it's not right, but they are required to believe it. If they try to assert their reality, the price is high. It's especially high if the mistake is theirs; that is, they didn't interpret correctly. So, when confused, they remain quiet, not knowing what's right. They no longer trust what they know. They accept their abuser's reality because they have likely been isolated or have no others in their life with whom they can discuss things. Even if they do, they don't, because that would be disloyal.

In the regular course of a day, an autistic person often feels confused by other people's actions. A person with PTSD also frequently interprets situations erroneously. With either diagnosis, the patient is at a higher susceptibility for gaslighting, both conscious and unconscious. Put the diagnoses together, and trust—of self or others—is ever more precarious.

Gaslighting it harmful—regardless of the reason it's employed. This is because it erases the person's experience. A lover who hurts their partner at home but praises or dotes on them in public has created a system whereby the partner is confused. What is love? What is safety? What is respect? What's true? Usually, these things are defined by the exploiter—and those definitions often change without notice. Their partner comes to doubt what they thought they knew. The abuser's reality is law. *And*, since someone with ASD/PTSD already has trouble with the world around them, they may not recognize when their world is being manipulated. Nod, "No." Shake, "Yes."

IV. Relationship with a narcissist

Being in a relationship with a narcissist can initially be thrilling. They can be very charming, coming on strong and making you believe you are the best thing to happen to them. They can appear to be the perfect partner. The world outside the home often sees them as intelligent, kind, and caring. They attend to you well in public, and you believe in the love. Maybe there is a teasing comment here or there, but you dismiss it as your partner's desire to help you be better. As time goes by, you begin to notice more things that don't seem right, but you can't put your finger on it. If you bring it up for discussion, you find out you were wrong, and you feel badly because you had questioned the narcissist's motives. You are reminded of all the wonderful things they've done and how they have been so supportive. You feel awful. (Note: Gaslighting is being used here.) You spend time questioning your own thinking and decide you made a wrong decision about the narcissist and you vow to be very careful about questioning their motives again. You find yourself doing things you wouldn't ordinarily do, acting in ways that go against your inner voice or value system. Narcissists are good at hijacking your sense of self; as they push you beyond healthy boundaries, you lose your personal power.

An autistic adult who is in the sights of a narcissist may be feeling like they belong for the very first time. Acceptance! Too good to be true! If the world sees the narcissist as intelligent, kind, and caring, many autistic adults will too. They may not have the social skills to ascertain the non-verbal body language for themselves, so they will count on the views of other people they trust. A narcissist is capable of fooling everyone.

There's no solid ground to stand on in a relationship with a narcissist. Just when you think you've got even a part of the relationship figured out, everything changes—and most likely it changes around an abusive act by the narcissist. Then the ground changes again and there's yet another traumatic experience to process. Processing the experiences becomes an exercise in futility because no matter what happened, the narcissist will change the story, you will be at fault, and then owe either an apology to the narcissist or have to do something you don't want to do to "make" things ok again. While that is all transpiring, and you know deep down inside that it wasn't your fault, you relent and either apologize or do what the narcissist wants, which deepens the confusion about what happened because why are you apologizing or doing something you don't want to do if it wasn't your fault? Eventually, the exploiter is so convincing you feel like you are an inherently bad person and wonder why they even put up with you! Having autism is a disadvantage in a relationship with a narcissist because in addition to processing speed, agreeability and forthrightness, there may already be a history of abuse, low self-esteem, and the need to be in a relationship so as to have the human contact that is so essential to living a healthy life.

V. Interpersonal violence (aka: domestic violence)

First, it's imperative for people to understand that interpersonal violence (IPV; also, often called "domestic violence") is not only about physical bruises and broken bones, though that's "easier" to prove. IPV is also about mental, verbal, and emotional abuse, sexual assault, financial exploitation, isolation, power, and control. It's the epitome of exploitation. Nevertheless, on the whole, people don't seem to understand IPV. This is evident by how we treat victims. In the USA, anyway, the most common question victims hear is "Why don't you leave?" It's such a shaming question, putting the onus on the victim and confirming their view that they are bad or stupid or hopeless. Nobody seems to ask why it's ok in our society for the abuser to abuse. Why not focus on stopping the abuse instead of just getting the victim away? Why not hold abusers accountable for their own actions?

MaryD writes:

In my experience, the general public has no idea what domestic abuse is. In an amalgamation of stories I've listened to, the following isn't even the tip of the iceberg:

It's not a question of leaving. It's that my work history has been sporadic, or I get paid so little I can't leave. It's about that my abuser has my paycheck put into his personal account; I have no access. It's about not having transportation to get myself to work, doctors, or support groups. It's about having bad credit due to all the bills "I" haven't paid, and being unable to pay the utility bill that was in my name, so I can't get electricity or oil in a new place. I certainly can't afford first and last month's rent to get into even a fleabag apartment. More than likely, I am estranged from friends and family due to the isolation my abuser enacted. I also don't have the energy or even understanding enough to "teach" others about abuse tactics. I am ashamed. I constantly hear that I should know better. I'm called a drama queen. I'm told I'm a coward because I'm male and my abuser is my wife, the "little lady." I'm blamed because I have an education or good finances or I'm good-looking, so I could do so much better. I've been told things like I must be a masochist because if I didn't like being abused, I wouldn't stay. I've been threatened and outed; I don't know what I think anymore; I have no self-confidence.

The policeman who came to my apartment after a particularly awful "fight" was initially ok. I was a mess, of course, and my abuser was calm and charming. The cop asked if I wanted to go to a shelter for abused women. I know this shelter. I declined. He got frustrated and started victim-blaming. He offered a homeless shelter for the night...for me! Why not my abuser? I didn't do anything, my abuser did! Further, the police person didn't understand that if I leave and go to the shelter, I can stay only for 30 days. Then I'm out, but to where? Yes, the advocates can help me with paperwork, but the housing assistance list has a five-year waiting list. (I feel pretty stupid, but even I know that five years is much *much* longer than 30 days!)

Heating assistance (provided I can find a place to rent on my $10/hr job) isn't awarded until the spring (note: after the harshest winter months have passed), and I trust myself so little that I'm sure I can't make good choices. I'm overwhelmed. *Then*, my abuser is blowing up my phone, making promises, apologizing, threatening suicide. I am tempted. If I return home, the abuse will probably get worse, but I don't know that at first. Then I feel even more stupid. So, I'll deny. It's safer that way anyway. I won't be stalked. I'll know exactly where my abuser is, so I can gauge the tension. When I don't know where they are, I'm always looking over my shoulder. The not knowing is far more antagonizing. I can't manage.

All of this is, of course, magnified if we share children and/or if there are animals in the household. My abuser has told me I'll lose my child if I go to a homeless shelter; I believe it. My mind is not my own. I also fear my pets will be hurt or killed, because they can't go with us.

I remember the look in my dog's eyes as he was being dragged by the tail out into the yard and beaten. The court system in my state favors parental rights to both parents at 50/50. This is a good thing, unless one parent is an abuser. The power lies with the parent who gets to say "no" to doctors, schools, sports, clubs, or any activity that might be nurturing to the child but inconvenient to the parent. I guess I never understood how, if one parent abuses the other, they can still be considered a good parent. Also, because we're gay, our child only has the DNA of one of us. I'm certain to lose custody because it's not my biological child. And abuse, without bruises or breaks, is so hard to prove. I fear that the child will be similarly abused and grow up feeling as unsafe as I do. Or worse yet, be turned against me. I can protect my child better if I have access to him all the time. And what of the threats made against other loved ones if I don't do as I'm told? All of this, to say nothing of where could I ever get the money to retain an attorney? I can't fight my abuser alone; I'm afraid. I shake just knowing we'll meet for custody drop off, even if it's in public. I certainly can't face him in court, about which he'll be really *really* mad.

The above experiences are quite common across all cognitive abilities. It can get worse, however, in neurodivergent populations, such as in ASD and PTSD. The communication, trust, fear, cooperation, and different processing speeds make attractive targets.

Lisa gives a list of features she has noticed that are specifically associated with an increased risk of abuse:

Vulnerable: It's the same old thing about how autistic people are vulnerable and easily taken advantage of and generally try to fit in. Autistic people miss hints, social cues, and can't always tell who to trust, so they believe what they are being told by an abuser and end up in an abusive relationship. The abuser works their charms at the beginning of the relationship to gain trust, and it's hard to think differently when the abuse starts, because it makes no sense and it's intermingled with charm and trust-retaining behaviors.

Lack of support: It's also hard to explain to other people when there aren't other people to explain it to...and then someone convinces you to go for help, only you don't know how. You try, and you get laughed at, so you go away, and then there's no one to help again. And, if you do have help, it's difficult to explain what's happening because what's happening is so convoluted and confusing. The abuser tells you that you deserve that punishment/abuse and is very convincing. People who want to help tell you you don't deserve this, but then blame you by saying things like, "God doesn't give you more than you can handle," "You made your bed, you have to lie in it," or "Pull yourself up by your bootstraps" (which, by the way, isn't physically possible). The abuser has examples and does circular arguing, a useful tactic to confuse people.

Aloneness: Sometimes being in an abusive relationship feels better than being alone when you know that loneliness can be such a deep, dark place. Also, I think with autistic people, they have spent a lot of time alone, so much so that just the opportunity of having a relationship is too much to pass up, making it easy to ignore the warning signs and be in denial that anything is wrong. Also, it makes leaving so hard.

Withdrawing: When/if you figure out you need help, and all you want to do is withdraw because you're hurting and confused, your partner can out-talk you, outsmart you, and present as a loving partner and friend such that it feels silly to ever think you needed help. (Note: Even my personal physician blamed me for the troubles we were having. He essentially told me to be a better wife, and explained with examples like bringing my husband his slippers and cooking his favorite foods!)

Fear: And, when you're scared because your abuser threatens you with all kinds of things if you step out of line, and you know it's true because you've crossed the line to check, even if it's just a couple of toes over the line and they prove they mean what they say, that produces fear. When the abuse is going to happen, is happening, or has happened there's this kind of numbness, not really feeling like you're a part of the world, or you just have so much inside your head you can't get anything out, so you act normal; you go to work the next day with a smile on your face, except for the worst one of all—you can't maintain a smile and a co-worker notices and helpfully berates you for not being "on" that day.

Passive: There's this thing inside you that just wants peace, so you learn to do whatever it takes to keep the peace, saying it's for your children, but it's really for you too. Then there are the times when they are going after the children, so you do something to make them angry, and then they're off them and onto you, but you at least succeeded in keeping them safe.

Masking: You're so good at masking that no one knows you're being abused, not even yourself. You doubly don't know who you are. You are who your abuser says you are, but even so, there's a masked person for the world to see, and somewhere; there's the real you; but for autistic people, they may have never met their real selves because they learned from a very early age to mask in order to fit in. It's a double whammy of self-identification gone wrong.

Change: It is beyond difficult to manage changes throughout the day for autistic people. When a schedule has an unexpected change, it floors an autistic person to where they may need to have time alone to regulate. Change is so repulsive that autistic people plan their day to the smallest detail in order to be successful in society. Change, like an appointment was cancelled, it rains, there's a substitute, an unexpected phone call, a new person joins the group, an unexpected piece of mail arrives, a relationship dies, or you forgot you had to get gas...are very difficult to manage, especially if more than one happens on the same day. Now, imagine quickly changing to a new, unfamiliar home, a new address, new rooms, odors, neighborhood, route to school/ work. The packing, the fear, the anxiety...are just debilitating. You are doing it mostly alone. There's a new kitchen, living room, window views, stores, playgrounds, sounds—nothing is the same.

Helpers need to be educated about the very different, complicated world in which the victim lives. They also need to know themselves well, including prejudices, expectations, and personality traits that could (and almost always do) re-victimize when they are unexplored.

MaryD writes:

In my past work as a domestic violence advocate, I took a training wherein the audience was made up of several public service professions such as advocates, nurses, police, teachers, and clergy. It was noted that one of the main difficulties in victims being able to report is the frequent proximity of the abuser. Many in the audience noted that victims were seldom left alone by the abuser. Thus, if a victim presented to an emergency room, the abuser would be with them. When the medical professional asked if there is violence at home, they would of course answer that there was not. Similarly, school personnel noted the ever-present technology and frequent texting used to control students/ victims. Police, too, though often separating an apparent feuding couple, are not always able to get one out of the eyesight of the other. Research has demonstrated that the closer the proximity to the authority figure, the more likely the disempowered will do what they are "supposed to do" (e.g., Milgram 1963). In fact, one nurse mentioned in training that he had succeeded in getting the abuser out of the room, though the abuser was still standing near the door, close enough to intimidate the victim. The nurse noted feeling frustrated because the victim, who had clearly been hurt purposefully, not only would not admit the abuse but upon leaving was overheard by the nurse whispering, "Don't worry, I didn't tell them anything." For the nurse, it was irritating to have "taken all that time to give her a shot at reporting." He blamed the victim for not taking the chance. Interpersonal abuse is not as easy as that.

In another hospital situation, a woman had fallen and hurt herself legitimately. She was taken to the hospital. Somehow, her estranged (abusive) husband had found out and arrived with typical bluster, giving orders and taking over his wife's care. The woman couldn't decline his visit; she was on auto- pilot and could barely speak, let alone give instructions. A nurse happened to have noticed the machines showing a marked increase in her heart and pulse activity. She calmly called security and had the man removed from the room and, eventually, the clinic. Safety is sometimes as easy as someone noticing.

VI. An important distinction between narcissistic and IPV abusers

In reading the above sections on narcissists and interpersonal violence, it might seem that the perpetrators of such abuse are the same. It is important to distinguish between the two kinds of exploitative perpetrators, however, as knowing the differences can help greatly when seeking services during recovery. In short, the motivations of narcissistic abusers are that they maintain the ideal of self-superiority in all aspects of life. It's who they are. They tend to have a very low (if any discernible) sense of empathy, yet can "perform" emotions when it suits them. They may appear confident, but they have a high need for validation, and almost anything they do involves seeking that validation. When something or someone challenges their sense of superiority, they become aggressive or enraged. Yet they often will have high impulse control, so they might smile through the perceived ego-assault; later will be hell for their victim. With a narcissist, because everything is about them, the relationship is never genuine.

While a narcissist is always abusive (should they not constantly have their ego stroked), not every abuser is a narcissist. Interpersonal violence, including domestic abuse, child abuse, bullying, and all other forms of person-to-person abuse, is a learned behavior. It results from the need to have power and control over others. It doesn't come from substance abuse or lack of sleep or being stressed at work. It's a choice to hurt others. And as long as those choices are working for the perpetrator, they will not change. IPV is characterized by chronic manipulation and rapidly changing emotions. A loving conversation can turn into a raging diatribe in a moment's time.

The need to control another (i.e., external control) is the issue in IPV, whereas with a narcissist, the drive is an internal mandate to feel superior. With an IPV abuser, there is a level of empathy, which means there can sometimes be room for them to change. Given that their bad behavior works well for them, however, chances are low. The victim can't "make them see reason." People only change when they're uncomfortable at length. Once an abuser can no longer get their selfish needs met within their comfort level, they will switch partners or change up a situation—still within the bubble of abuse. (Note: IPV victims beware: You *cannot* meet an abusive person's needs. Their displeasure is not about you not working hard enough. They aren't pleased with you when you work yourself to death in the relationship; they're pleased with themselves for having such power...for pulling those strings...for the fear in your eyes...for the major kick it is to control others.)

In order to change, an abuser has to take control of themselves—not of their victim (Bancroft 2002). That means they need to engage professional help that will aid them in exploring their internal processes. Though change is possible, it's also a difficult and long process. They need to stick with a change program and really engage. With a narcissistic abuser, the current perception is that they are generally not capable of change because they cannot introspect their behavior. The narcissism reaches deep into their personality, and it relies on the *perception* of superiority (not necessarily the truth of it). Facing themselves realistically is in direct opposition to what their ego demands.

The above is the tip of the iceberg relating to IPV and abusers versus narcissists. If seeking services, one should be certain their professional fully understands the mechanisms involved in narcissism, abuse, and surviving it. It's such a complicated journey that engaging helpers who aren't trained in this area could end up hurting you on yet another level. Regardless of the kind of abuser you have, however, remember that *abuse is abuse*—there's no good reason for it...not pity or fatigue...not bad childhoods or previous wounds...and certainly not love.

Chapter VIII

Challenges in Recognizing Interpersonal Abuse in ASD

What is interpersonal abuse in ASD?

Interpersonal abuse experienced by people of all abilities along the autism spectrum is vast and often difficult to discern. While many forms of abuse are easily observable, there need not be a specifically recognizable incident or assault in order for trauma to occur. There are other, more subtle, chronic, harmful ways autistic people are abused socially, emotionally, and mentally. There are also many aspects leading to abuse going unnoticed, including the inherent characteristics of autism, autistic people themselves not always understanding what an abusive situation feels like, and cultural differences between autistic and non-autistic people.

Frequently, social situations leave autistic people with discouraging feelings of being different, not fitting in, being ostracized, and misunderstood—so much so that when an abusive situation arises, an autistic person may not recognize it; they may assume it's another uncomfortable social situation. Abuse for autistic people can be subtle, outright, emotional, physical, by whole groups, or just one person at a time. The abuse can happen once in a day or multiple times a day, by the same people or various people. It can be perpetrated by strangers, caretakers, family, and acquaintances, some who abuse knowingly and many who are unaware that their actions have harmed. Each instance is a type of abuse with the possibility of developing into PTSD or other trauma-related disorders.

I. ASD/NT interactions

Studies using magnetic resonance imaging (MRI) have shown different structures in the brains of autistic people in comparison to non-autistic people (Ha *et al.* 2015). Knowing this information, it can be concluded that autistic people will be different than non-autistic people, especially in the areas of communication. Different, not less-than, not defective, not unworthy—just different.

Yet, autistic people regularly experience interpersonal abuse when they are expected to act like non-autistic people and are rejected and/or ostracized if they don't. The abuse can start very early for autistic children, as they are deemed different and bullied as early as kindergarten. As we saw in Chapter 7, autistic kids typically cannot process fast enough to escape. Also, they generally can't interpret others' motivation or put themselves first. Thus, when teachers or caretakers hold beliefs such as, "kids should work it out themselves," they can be doing a great disservice to the autistic child. The emotional damage due to chronic bullying, rejection, and not fitting in can create a constant fear of social situations such that neurotransmitters related to stress are firing continually, causing the limbic system to employ its defenses with little or no relief. This can lead to mental health issues such as anxiety, depression, obsessive-compulsive disorder, or PTSD.

The challenge is recognizing the impact that harmful behavior has on an autistic child due to their atypical reaction to being harmed. Non-autistic children tend to react in an obviously emotionally distraught way when bullied or treated unfairly.

An autistic child, however, generally reacts in one of two ways: they withdraw, not communicating their feelings (possibly due to alexithymia) and go unnoticed by people who can help them; or they go into meltdown stage, where they are explicit in their feelings but blamed for them rather than helped through them. These reactions can go on for days, months, and years even; autistic people can become accustomed to being treated this way, and not recognize abusive situations as they experience them at work, in public, and/or at home. Many autistic adults learn to discern abusive situations as they experience more of the world, and either become advocates to help other autistic people, or stay in abusive situations not knowing how to get out. Either way, many are left with countless traumatic interactions piling up.

II. Myths

Another way autistic people can experience abuse is through myths. Myths are common ideas people have about ASD that are not only untrue, but highly damaging as well. They can cause high expectations and put unfair burdens on autistic people to the point where they are misunderstood so completely that the loneliness and exclusion become too much to bear.

Myth 1: Autism is a childhood condition

This myth results in people not believing autism in adults is real. This myth indicates that the condition is resolvable, or that adults don't have ASD brains. Research identifying autism as a structural, neurological condition abounds. Though early intervention can help in skills development, one does not "grow out of" autism. This is a dangerous myth, too, because it prevents so many ASD people from securing services or accommodations, particularly once they age into adulthood. Further, autistic people trying to help themselves live fulfilling lives will be hindered if asking for services is met with disdain, accusations of non-compliance, and unjust assumptions.

Myth 2: Autistic people don't want to have friends

One of the leading characteristics of autism is difficulty with social communication. In the neurotypical world, it is a personal choice to have friends or not, how many to have, and when to spend time with them. For an autistic person, these are not always choices. Making and maintaining friendships can be elusive and cumbersome. It's not that autistic individuals don't want them; they just struggle with the concept. Friendships are complicated; it makes the whole experience more difficult if the autistic person has been unfairly judged as being antisocial and uncaring about wanting to connect with people in meaningful ways.

Also, because the autistic person might need solitary time, or turn inward when confused, or because they don't generally communicate well, many helpers assume they don't need friends. This could not be further from the truth. Because the neurotypical world is so confusing on a regular basis, and often causes autistic people to feel apart from others naturally, having friends to count on, who understand and regard them positively, is essential. Turning inward and staying silent are more often signals of confusion or sadness rather than self-sufficiency.

Myth 3: Autistic people are savants and have special talents

Many autistic adults have special passions in which they become experts, but it's less about genius and more about being so engrossed in their passion that they learn everything about it. When they are expected to be savants, and then fall short, they can experience rejection of their autism and humiliation from not measuring up to another's expectations. As an adult, this feeds into all the times they experienced a situation like this growing up, so they are not just feeling the result of this interaction; they are most likely feeling every past instance when something like this happened to them. It is chronic abuse over time.

Myth 4: We are all a little autistic

This myth is harmful in many ways. It devalues the experiences of a person who is actually autistic. It is demeaning to autistic people, who struggle daily with the multiple and complicated aspects of autism, such that each day can be so challenging, making it to the end feels like a great accomplishment was achieved. The thought that "we are all a little autistic" indicates a belief that autism exists in little pieces. It doesn't. It's an all-around, 24/7 brain structure that affects all parts of life, every day. "A little autistic" also feels like NTs are judging autistic people negatively for not being able to do what they can do. It is highly disrespectful in that the levels of unfairness, lack of validation, and that old feeling of rejection and not fitting in, are extreme. It feels like yet another indication of being less-than, not belonging, and failure for not measuring up to the ever-elusive ideal of "normal."

Reaction

The above examples of myths, abusive situations, and the resulting sense of invalidation are important to understand because, in autistic people, hurtful situations and abuse often go unnoticed. For many, their first reaction is to withdraw, leave the situation, and possibly even believe what has been revealed to them about themselves. This leaves them alone with conflicting feelings of their worth. Another reaction is to mask (remember that while autistic people mask to fit in, they also mask to not show how they feel inside). It makes recognizing abuse difficult when deep emotional reactions to interpersonal abuse are hidden behind a mask.

For many autistic people, reaching out for help is painful, scary, confusing, and often creates even more agitation. Professionals typically assess how a patient/client presents when they arrive for help. They have no way of knowing the person they are helping is autistic unless it is disclosed, so the professionals will be assessing based on neurotypical standards of distress. A negative experience can transpire from the miscommunication of professionals interpreting autistic behaviors using their knowledge of non-autistic people. This can result in misdiagnosis, unnecessary tests, misunderstandings, unfair assumptions, and/or minimizing symptoms. In fact, recent research reveals a stunningly high number of female autistics are misdiagnosed (Muller 2019). This is particularly important for currently middle-to-late age women for whom the ASD diagnosis didn't exist in their youth. This has resulted in a long-term misdiagnosis towards issues such as bipolar disorder, borderline personality disorder, and obsessive-compulsive disorder, to name a few.

Lisa shares:

If I had been diagnosed earlier than 47 years old, my life would be completely altered. To start with, knowing I was different from my peers as young as first grade led to a strong belief that I was less-than. The belief was cemented in my mind by the teasing, bullying, and rejection I endured while growing up, which continued into adulthood. This is a mindset I can still struggle with today if I don't regularly check in with myself. Then, I believe, everything else that followed in terms of negative experiences came from that mindset.

III. Social interactions

As difficult as social interactions can be for an autistic adult, many still want to make connections and have friendships. But friendship isn't a static thing; it is dynamic, fluid, and often vague. This presents great challenges to autistic people. There are an infinite number of possibilities of social interactions, which might sound exciting or surprising to an NT, but which leave an enormous potential for misunderstandings.

There are many ways misunderstandings within a friendship can be hurtful to an autistic person. The first is from expectations. Neurotypical people have expectations regarding any specific friendship. There may be expectations of honesty, loyalty, time spent together, understanding, and support, to name just a few. A big difficulty with vocabulary is the very good chance that the definitions of those expectations are different for autistic people than they are for non-autistic people. The discrepancies of the definitions can result in one of the two friends feeling hurt and—depending on what happens—being abused. Also, it's more than likely the autistic person gets hurt because everything becomes so confusing. For example, someone may say, "That smells so good!" and actually mean they want to try some. If the autistic person misses that cue and doesn't share, they will likely feel awful they weren't "a good friend" or that they were rude. When an autistic person says, "That smells so good!" they actually mean it smells good. That's it. Nothing else. Easy. These language differences can cause feelings of alienation. Misunderstandings can also come from assumptions about the meanings of words.

Lisa shares:

> When I write texts or emails to people, there are times when my words have been taken to have an underlying message or a double meaning. The message can be interpreted as malicious and hurtful, when I am actually

trying to be diplomatic. For example, once I was trying to work out a school situation for one of my children. The teacher was emailing me in such vague terms there was no clear meaning and, I thought, I was replying in a very direct manner such that there could be no misunderstanding of what I was saying. I was eventually invited to come in and visit with the principal, where I was told that the teacher felt threatened by my correspondence, and so I would be communicating only with the principal from now on. I told her I didn't understand and suggested the school wasn't being responsive to my concerns. I was only being intentionally direct and to the point so there would be no miscommunication. The teacher read a completely different email because she was looking for messages between the lines and hidden meanings. The principal said, "I'm sorry you feel that way, but I'm going to support my teachers."

I couldn't figure out what I was saying wrong, or why I couldn't get through to ostensibly learned people! I needed to help my child, so I figured out that it was time to consider whether or not to disclose my autism.

Disclosing ASD

Disclosure is a personal decision based on individual experiences, reasons, and potentially dismissive responses. Usually the decision to disclose a diagnosis of ASD is based on a situation where the possible negative response outweighs the desirable positive response. As always there is the potential for an abusive situation, whether deliberate or unwitting.

Lisa shares:

I had suspected for years that I was autistic. I knew in my heart that my social confusion and failure to connect with people was because there was something different about me and after I learned about autism, I knew that was the reason. I didn't tell anyone, until one day I ventured tentatively with the smallest possible disclosure. I told a person I trusted at the time that I thought I was similar to autistic people. I was given a resounding "NO!" That sense of rejection and dismissal was so strong, and my embarrassment about my fragility so hurtful, that I didn't bring it up again for years.

Typically, I choose to keep both ASD and PTSD diagnoses private to me. If I am overwhelmed enough to disclose my diagnosis, I need understanding. My reasoning is the disclosure will explain why I'm having such a difficult time, instead of me appearing incompetent, lazy, or full of excuses. More often than not, however, my hopes are dashed when I observe the responses. I've had a person give me a blank stare for a few seconds, and then go on with what we were doing as if I didn't say anything at all. I've had a person smile and say something along the lines of "If I can do this, so can you," or smile awkwardly and just leave me standing there as soon as humanly possible. Another response is to tell me, "If you'd just try harder, then you could manage it; look, everyone else is doing fine." I have received instantaneous dismissal even from people who have known me for a while and still can't grasp my disclosure of autism. It's not a disease! It is a structural neurological difference in our brains.

While I recognize that responses like these are not from a place of listening and understanding, neither are they from a place of malice. These responses are from people who are trying to "fix" a problem they do not understand and that does not need to be "fixed" by them. It occurs to me often that the problem to be fixed looks different to NTs than it does to us autistic people. NTs are focusing on our being different, and they're looking at the differences as burdensome. As an autistic person, I see the problem as the NTs being unable to slow down and stretch their thinking. It is time for people to listen and really hear what an autistic person is saying to them. It's time to respectfully encourage more disclosure to learn about autism. It's not a time for saying the first thing that comes to mind, proposing meaningless solutions or encouragement by way of relating. The only people who can really relate are other autistic adults or possibly people who have listened closely with their ears open and truly tried to understand, not for themselves, but for the autistic person standing before them.

Of all the responses, the one that leaves me loneliest after disclosing my diagnosis is the one where I actually tell someone I'm overwhelmed and why, and I tell them what I need, and they suggest exactly the opposite. Rather than help me find a quiet area or allow me to take time on my own, they've said things like, "Oh, you hate people," or "You can handle it if I can handle it." I then know I haven't been heard or understood—at all. This, in turn, feeds into old memories of rejection, misunderstandings, and hurt, which leads to flashbacks where I don't just *remember* the memories, I *relive* them.

IV. Employment

The interview process is not designed for autistic people in that interviews typically require small talk and other expectations of social communication which are not ASD strengths. Autistic people also tend to answer the exact question asked, without elaboration. They aren't readily able to read body language and so many miss important cues. Higher than usual anxiety can also cause them to freeze. Nevertheless, autism is only a different way of brain function; most are as capable as others in performing the job. Still, the fear caused by multiple interviewers, strange environments, and unknown questions inhibits an ASD interviewee's ability to respond quickly or accurately.

These actions can meet with reproachful looks or dismissal from uninformed interviewers, and rejection—for how the interviewee exhibits rather than what they know—can be yet another discrediting experience. Another reminder of them being valued as less-than and/or not fitting in. Autistic people who can successfully manage to get through the interview process are just beginning a journey through the work environment, also developed for the utmost success of non-autistic people.

Once employed, various types of office politics also provide challenges for non-neurotypical staff. Office politics is defined as: the process and behavior in human interactions involving power and authority. It is an autistic employee's nightmare come true: "human interactions involving power and authority." Whether it be gossip, disgruntled employees, jealous teammates, or forms of harassment, autistic people in general are vulnerable to the negative aspects of social interactions. Apart from politics, there are many ways an autistic employee can be hurt. First, just understanding the conversations around office politics can keep an autistic employee off balance emotionally and reduce their productivity. Autistic people generally do not gossip; they can be blatantly honest, but any comment will most likely be said in the moment, not later, behind closed doors or others' backs. Many autistic people do not understand complex social situations and find themselves feeling anxious, overwhelmed, and frustrated. While many autistic people tend to avoid partaking in social discussions at work and concentrate on doing their job, they are still affected by office politics through co-workers' jealousy, having their work ethics exploited, and any possible advancement through promotions being based on "who you know" instead of job performance.

Regarding job performance, work reviews for autistic people tend to be unfairly based on non-autistic behavior. When compared to their colleagues, autistic employees can easily fall short on "fitting in," being a team player, and cooperating on projects, even though they are doing their very best to accomplish all that. The boss may also give a poor review based on time management, communication, not showing initiative, or even working independently.

Autistic employees may be held to unreasonable expectations for their neurotype. The abuse can come into play if they are fired, are dealt with harshly, or receive a pay cut based on inaccurate expectations.

The reasons an autistic person can be a valuable employee are all directly related to autism. Loyalty to the workplace, attention to details, high standards, creative problem-solving, rule following, and not being highly sociable are all aspects of a good employee and characteristics of autism. Employers who have an autistic person on their staff working at a job they love would do well to support them as valuable assets to the team.

V. Sexual abuse

Sexual abuse in the autistic population is reported to occur at substantially higher rates than in their neurotypical counterparts. Issues such as consent, communication, agreeableness, lack of knowledge, perceived asexuality, desire to be included, and a disinclination of authority to address reports of sexual assault contribute to the sexual exploitation of ASD people. Any one of these issues is challenging in and of itself; compound them and "overwhelmed" doesn't begin to cover what can happen.

An early risk factor setting up an ASD person for sexual assault is a lack of sexual knowledge. Studies show that parents can fall short in discussing sex and its attendant issues with their autistic child, perhaps for reasons such as fear of encouraging them towards sexual activity or bias in terms of their ability to raise children of their own. What's more, perhaps due to their own discomfort, parents often discuss sex and sexuality in vague terms, using euphemisms such as "the birds and the bees," "hoo haa," and other non-direct idioms. They tend to instruct with words rather than pictures or props, and many rush through the presentation, leaving less time for processing and questions than is needed. Thus, early formal training falls short. In addition, whereas most neurotypical children get a lot of information from peers and teachers, autistic kids tend to be isolated and/or ridiculed for interests they may have in this area.

Second comes the complication of consent. Consent in this case is typically viewed as an agreement between two people about doing something particular. Though it is in essence a negotiation regarding boundaries—like/dislike, risk/benefit—consent often happens informally between partners, with no mediators or signed formal agreements. This introduces many levels of complication for an autistic person. For example, autistic people have spent much of their lives having their rights to self-determination being ignored or violated. Thus, the reference point for personal boundaries is often not well understood, causing the person to doubt or misunderstand personal space. Second, consent uses communication expressed via verbal and body language and social cues. This puts an autistic person at a distinct disadvantage as poor communication tends to be a core component of ASD. Also, once the person has agreed, should something happen in the encounter that is not ok, the autistic person will often consider the initial agreement as resolute and not know they can say "no." Fear of rejection or being pressured to couple up adds to the confusion. All of this is not to mention the amount of energy it takes to consider consent, behavioral options, or possible sensory dysregulation involved in sexual activities.

Social mimicry also puts the autistic person at risk. This is a behavior wherein the autistic person, in an attempt to mask their "deficiencies" will copy the behavior of people around them so as to appear "normal." Though they may not know the messages they're putting out aside from "I'm like you are," the person with whom they're talking may interpret it as flirting and interest. Because autism often prevents them from interpreting others' intentions, the person with autism may not know they're in danger until far too late. And then, due to traits like cooperativeness or processing speed, they are unable to decline further activity.

Lastly, predation is an ever-present threat to autistic people. In the USA general population, statistics commonly present that one in three females and one in six males are sexually assaulted at some point in their lives. Sexual assault is an epidemic even before we break down the numbers for autism. In a twins study regarding the sexual assault of autistic women, results indicated that autistic women were three times more likely to experience sexual assault than their non-autistic twin (Ohlsson *et al.* 2018). ASD makes a person extra-vulnerable as autistic people are socially alone, quiet, and uninformed. In addition, due to the possible need for help in the home or community, autistic people are far more exposed to outsiders operating in susceptible places.

MaryD writes:

Many years ago, a newly divorced acquaintance (who is autistic) once came to my house for tea. As we were talking, she began to ask me questions about plumbers and what kind of gratuities she should give them when they came to her house. Initially, I thought we were having a conversation about plumbers and gratuities. Her questions, however, raised concerns. For example, she wanted to know about extra gratuity for weekend visits and how often they should come for follow-up visits. That stuck out to me, so I asked more pointed questions. It happened that she had a kitchen sink issue that her ex-partner used to take care of. He told her to call a plumber, which she did. After he fixed the sink, he told her a convincing story about how housewives gave

> gratuities. Before she knew it, he had raped her. He then returned for two more "follow-up visits." Though the situation was very distressing to her, her major concern was making sure she was following the rules and treating the worker right.

Having read the above, those with empathy and compassion may wonder how to help this ever-increasing population. Research, which focuses the bulk of its efforts on autism in children and adolescents, is continually facing budget cuts while answering mandates for new or updated information. Given that the World Health Organization (2019) estimates that worldwide, 1 in 160 children have autism, research must continue. There is no best guess estimate of adults with autism, particularly since the diagnosis was not well known before the early 1990s. Nevertheless, people of all ages in all walks of life are affected. Indeed, to borrow an idea from Public Services International:[1]

> The cost of [practicing awareness of the person before you] does not justify the deprivation of persons with autism to [realize their basic human rights].

How we as a people can do that is by recognizing that all people are valuable, all contribute to global diversity, and all have a basic right to self-determination. This right has often been perverted, ignored, or otherwise denied to many persons, both non-autistic and autistic. Thus, here is a brief reminder of what the United Nations declares as every person's right to development; that all persons are "entitled to participate in, contribute to, and enjoy economic, social, cultural and political development, in which all human rights and fundamental

---

1   www.world-psi.org/en/towards-autonomy-and-self-determination-persons-autism

freedoms can be fully realized" (UN Declaration on the Right to Development, proclaimed in 1986).

Benedict (2018) describes the "Basic Human Rights for Self-Development" as follows:

1. I have the right to have these Basic Human Rights and to stand up for them.

2. I have the right to have my needs and feelings be as important as anyone else's.

3. I have the right to experience and express my feelings, if I choose to do so, in a respectful way.

4. I have the right to not be responsible for the feelings of another.

5. I have the right to express my opinions, if I choose to do so, in a respectful way.

6. I have the right to set my own priorities.

7. I have the right to establish independence if I choose to.

8. I have the right to decide how I spend my time.

9. I have the right to choose my own lifestyle so long as I do not violate the rights of others.

10. I have the right to change my lifestyle, myself, my behaviors, my values, my life situation, and my mind.

11. I have the right to make honest mistakes and to admit those mistakes without feeling humiliated.

12. I have the right to self-fulfillment through my own talents and interests.

13. I have the right to grow as a person and to accept new challenges.

14. I have the right to choose with whom I spend my time and with whom I share my body.

15. I have the right to be treated with dignity and respect in all my relationships.

16. I have the right to be listened to respectfully.

17. I have the right to ask for what I want assertively.

18. I have the right to say "I don't understand" or "I don't know" without feeling or being humiliated.

19. I have the right to say "No" and to set limits and boundaries without feeling guilty.

20. I have the right to set limits on how I will be treated in relationships.

21. I have the right to expect my boundaries to be respected.

22. I have the right to walk away from toxic or abusive relationships.

Chapter IX

First Responders and Other Professionals

I. First, do no harm

It's important to recognize that first responders and other professionals likely have great motivation to be useful in improving a patient's or client's life circumstances. Providers in the helping professions are there to help people, and do not set out to intentionally hurt their charges. That being said, autistic people are prone to many more unintentional hurts and incidents of abuse than are neurotypical people. In advocating for "First, do no harm," one must be able to look realistically at what exactly does cause harm in the course of a normal business day.

Here Lisa gives is an example of doing harm (Dr. L.) and doing no harm (Dr. G.):

I went to my first visit to a psychiatrist with a bit of trepidation of the unknown, yet with an open mind, and hope we would connect in a positive way. My introduction to Dr. L. was of her telling me about herself. She talked about the prestigious college she graduated from, her successful practice in NYC, and how well she helps her clients.

Then, I was told I had to answer a questionnaire about myself that would go at a good pace and to answer as honestly as possible. The questionnaire was full of inquiries about medical history, childhood, marriage, traumas from the past, and more. Dr. L. didn't look at me as she started asking the questions and wrote down my answers. She didn't look at me as she continued to fire the questions at me. She just typed and went to the next question as fast as possible.

Meanwhile, I was answering as honestly as possible like she asked me to do. I started feeling more and more anxious as the questions brought up traumatic memories from my past. My anxiety heightened to a level where tears came and I was trying to regulate myself and still answer question after question about very difficult times in my life. I'm sure Dr. L. could hear the anxiety in my shaky voice, could tell I was in tears, yet she relentlessly kept up the rapid pace of questions. Many of you may be thinking, "Why didn't you speak up?" I couldn't. Due to the neurological makeup of my autistic mind, the more anxiety I experience, the quieter I am. My behavior in those instances could be mistaken as being ok by non-autistic people. My emotions don't typically heighten to the point of a physical meltdown, where it would become obvious that I need help. I get quiet. The quieter I am, the more anxiety I feel, the less I can communicate. It's during the times I get very quiet that I need the most help, but I don't receive it because many doctors (both physical health providers and mental health providers) just see me as a calm non-autistic person, not as the suddenly overly quiet, struggling autistic person I am in that moment. I need to be seen as an autistic adult. I need doctors to know I will not behave like a non-autistic person, yet even when they know of my differences, they continue to communicate with me as if I am neurotypical. They don't meet me where I am.

The problem with my experience with that questionnaire was not remembering the traumas that were brought up—but that I was reliving the traumas as if they had just happened due to PTSD. I felt as if I had just been through multiple traumas and was left with memories overlapping and swirling around together in my thoughts. I really hoped that when the questions were done Dr. L. would help me to regulate, to bring my anxiety down, and to talk a bit about how to feel safe again. I was wrong.

When she was finished, she looked at me and said, "I have the authority to hospitalize you and keep you there until I feel you are ready to leave." Dr. L. might as well have said she was going to put me in prison without due process and throw away the key. I was horrified. Her words became seared in my mind. I will always remember that statement. I do know it set me back weeks in my journey to health and healing. I found it very difficult to trust anyone trying to help me. I couldn't regulate my anxiety, my depression deepened, and I felt at any time Dr. L., who I had just met, could take me away from my children and I could be gone from them as long as she saw fit. I felt there was no place that was safe (not even my own home), and that there was nothing I could do about it. Who would believe me over her? Unfortunately for me, due to the way the medical office works, she was the only doctor I could see; there were no other options. I had to go back to see her if I wanted help.

Thankfully my psychologist, Dr. G., understands autistic clients, and I was able to process that horrible appointment with her. Dr. L. and Dr. G. have diametrically opposed philosophies on how to relate to me. One positive way Dr. G. communicates with me is to allow me to be who I am, an educated professional who has experienced multiple traumatic situations throughout my life. She doesn't patronize me, talk condescendingly, or think I can't help myself. She has confidence in me. She recognizes my strengths, helps me to see things in a healthier way when I can't, and has never wavered from her belief in my own ability to cope as she guides me. Dr. G. listens, she hears me, and has become someone I trust.

One reason for the open communication I experience with Dr. G. is she accepts my autism. She doesn't dismiss it, misunderstand it, or use it as "the problem" as other doctors have done. The reason it is so important that she accepts me as an autistic adult is then she and I can honestly understand each other. Dr. G. knew, from her own previous knowledge of autism and from listening to me, how I best communicated. If I needed the music in her office to be turned down, she gladly complied to help me be comfortable. I can think much clearer without the distracting background noise, even if it's just a soothing melody. We talked and she understands I'm very sensitive to perfumes and essential oils, and she made her office a safe place for me to be, sensory-wise. I could relax, take off my social mask, and be myself. Open, honest, and trusting—our client/doctor relationship is exactly where I need it to be emotionally for her to be able to help me. Dr. G. continues to be the essential person I trust as I continue on my journey towards health and healing. Because of this, I am not using energy to battle the environment or to teach someone how to relate to me. I can use that energy to be challenged with exploring things about me and learning new ways of doing things.

So, the time leading up to the second appointment with Dr. L. was a time of trying to come to terms with this new behavioral health provider and planning ahead for when I saw her again. The day of the appointment I went in and sat down. The greeting went smoothly, only to quickly fall apart on her first question to me—"Did you try the new med?" As an autistic adult, change is very difficult for me, and I hadn't been able to try the new medicine. I had previously told her it would be difficult for me and I didn't really want to take any medicine at all, although I understood it was necessary for me to process everything that had happened leading up to my husband's death, his suicide, and the aftermath.

This is what she told me—verbatim: "I'm not going to go to your house and shove them down your throat." Again, I felt very unsafe that she had even thought something like that and my anxiety went very high. All I could think was, "She might come to my home." She stared at me until I couldn't be there anymore and I said I needed to go and regulate myself. She agreed and I left. I found myself in my car, unable to drive home safely, until I brought my anxiety down to a manageable level with Dr. G.'s help.

In conclusion, I've had wonderful experiences with different types of both healthcare and mental healthcare providers. They usually are providers who listen to me and really hear me, which requires putting aside any preconceived notions about me or what malady brought me to their office. It requires accepting who I am as an autistic adult with sensory needs and autistic traits. Hearing enables putting what I'm saying to the doctor in context with my medical history, getting a sense of the big picture out of the details, and the ability to ask the right questions.

Lisa shares how for others with ASD/PTSD, as well as the professionals who help them, it might be important to know the following:

These were my two default states for a long time—invisible or bullied. I believed for many years of my life that the abuse, fear, and sadness were my fault because I was different. As I pass the half-century mark, I'm starting to realize I did nothing wrong. I didn't bully back. All I wanted was a friend or two, so if I could show kindness to someone, I did. Those kindnesses often ended up being used as a source for exploitation.

Thus, it would be helpful to a client or patient if the professional was aware that their clients or patients, "might have limited perception," might not have a repertoire of social knowledge, might have a history of being used or persecuted...and they might be masking well enough to appear basically normal, but coming closer and closer to exhausted. When providers are trying to work fast or are perhaps uncomfortable with a situation, the person before them—the actual person—can become invisible; perhaps the helper's mindset becomes mechanical as they rush to make a meeting or finish the day. Absentmindedness or complacency can cause a lot of damage.

As MaryD reveals:

> I was working with a client for four years. She had made substantial progress and was entering into a life-changing situation. It was a rough day for me, and I didn't take any time to breathe or check in with myself before I opened the door to her. Apparently, she was trying to tell me something, and I responded poorly. I didn't know it at the time. She cancelled the next appointment, and I didn't see her again for many months. She would not respond to my contacts. When we finally ran into each other, she dressed me down. I had no idea what I'd done, but it was—for her—enough to cut off all contact. Regardless of what we'd experienced of each other over those four years, my absent-ness lost her trust. What she'd perceived from that last session was far more than was in my notes. She wasn't hallucinating; something had certainly happened, and it lay squarely with me. In listening to her, I realized that I had not been fully present in the session and that I'd been complacent about her person-hood. I was horrified—and thankful. Had she decided not to confront me, as would be understandable, I'd never have known.

Indeed, many providers might never know the hurt they've caused. Some of that hurt is surmountable with time and support, some remains, and some goes on to infect future experiences. It's inevitable, given individual perceptions and unique inputs from various environments or challenging needs, that some will feel hurt, insulted, or unimportant.

Nevertheless, for a person to feel this way as a result of absentmindedness or complacency is certainly avoidable. Getting out of our own heads and seeing the unique individual before us, being open-minded about what they're telling us—both verbally and behaviorally—goes a long way towards understanding. This brings up the treatment strategy of developing cultural competence for the autistic person with PTSD.

II. Practical skills

Without an understanding of an autistic person's experiences in crisis or overwhelming situations, first responders are in danger of missing opportunities to help them or may even be causing them harm. Recognizing an overwhelming situation or crisis in an autistic person is imperative to begin interacting, communicating, and helping. Autistic people enduring a traumatic incident may not present the same way as others, even when compared to other autistic people. First responders and other helpers need to understand that while traumas such as dangerous, life-threatening situations are indeed distressful for autistic people, the chronic day-to-day interactions within a society that rejects them can be just as distressing, leading to a personal crisis. If first responders and other helpers do not understand practical skills in communicating with autistic people, medical doctors may not get the correct information, clergy could misunderstand their follower's needs, emergency medical technicians may fight a patient unnecessarily, lawyers won't seek the right outcome, and victim advocates may never truly serve their autistic clients. This is not just an inconvenience;

if practical skills are not part of the training of first responders and other helpers, autistic people can be harmed emotionally, mentally, and/or physically.

Understanding what you see: reality check

In many situations, certain autistic behaviors (e.g., acute agitation, maladaptive oppositional behavior), and "disturbing" activities (e.g., head banging and screaming) can be perceived by professionals as indicators of an autistic person being in crisis. In most cases, however, the actual crisis comes *after* the "helper's" (poor) response to those autistic behaviors. In short, the "disturbing" activities could be efforts to communicate. The autistic person may be trying to communicate their need for help or why they are so distraught, but they are often directed to stop those behaviors. Indeed, some people count the cessation of those behaviors as successes. They aren't. When a behavior used to communicate is misidentified as the problem and those behaviors are quashed, the autistic client can't get the help they need and so acts in true maladaptive ways, having no other option.

Just think for a moment; you have had a difficult morning and you just got stung by a bee. You fear an allergic reaction, and, for you, it is quickly becoming a crisis situation. You want to tell your friends, but you can't. No words will come out. You start jumping in front of them, trying to talk, waving your arms all over the place, and running around the room. What if your friends, who are not comfortable with your behavior, make you sit in a chair, use harsh voices, and to keep you safe, hug your arms to your side? Are you going to react in an increasingly aggressive manner? Probably. It would be understandable. If people only focus on the behavior instead of what you were actually trying to communicate, suddenly you're deemed "in crisis" because your behavior is deemed inappropriate. Thus, they misunderstand, and you're then forced to undergo grueling types of therapy to "teach you" better ways to respond the next time you act out, warranted or not. So much for the bee sting. In reality, the problem was how your friends reacted to your attempt at communicating, not the arm waving.

Current needs: in the moment

Given the rapid rate at which people with autism are being identified, and that it is such a diverse disorder, we need ever-more research. A review of the literature identified calls for investigation into areas such as early intervention, psychiatric comorbidities, biological basis, transitioning into adulthood, and experimental therapies. This is all good and very important. Research also takes time and money, and results are particular. What's suggested now is for professionals such as first responders, medical staff, school administration, and community providers to develop the "practical skills" so many studies ask for under the "Future directions" sections. In order to begin developing those skills, we need first to know how to recognize (or at least suspect) an autistic client.

Similar features of potentially autistic clients

The common saying is: "If you've met one autistic client, you've met one autistic client." Indeed, with the many known possible features of autism identified in the *DSM-V* (APA 2013), there are thousands of different symptom combinations that can manifest in autism. Thus, one ASD person does not present the same as another. Fortunately, there are some indicators that occur more often than others, and a caretaker can strengthen their education by looking for the following possible signs:

- talking over you and/or apparently ignoring social "rules" about personal space

- little or no eye contact

- lack of spontaneity

- vocal inflection is blunted or flat

- responding negatively to touch, noise, smells, or other environmental stimulation

- repetitive mannerisms

- responses that may seem "off" from what you're talking about

- sudden verbal silence

- restricted focus

- extended knowledge about specific subjects

- lack of friendships

- small or no social support network

- difficulty regulating emotion

- extreme response to sudden changes or surprises.

III. Cultural competency

The process of fully embracing our ignorance is transformative; otherwise, we try to control others' behavior so we don't feel helpless. Such embracing moves toward trust.

(van der Kolk in MacPherson 2018)

Cultural competency is "a set of congruent behaviors, attitudes, and policies that allow us to function effectively in cross-cultural situations" (Cross *et al.* 1989, p.13). Unbeknownst to many, cultures are not just about race, ethnicity, or religion. Families have cultures, offices have cultures, there's even a culture for elevators. *Culture* includes patterns of beliefs, actions, customs, and values, among other things. *Competency* is about the degree to which one functions effectively in a given situation. To be culturally competent, therefore, is to be able to effectively understand, communicate, and interact with others from outside your own social group. Its development exponentially increases the chances of respectful, fruitful interactions between parties. It's a dynamic process, however, and needs constant review.

Self-awareness is the foundation of cultural competency. It isn't about how another person is different but, rather, what we can do to understand them. It's "us" oriented, that is, knowing ourselves as a means of understanding different neurotypes. Being culturally competent is about having an open mind with a curiosity for learning about the self, including the ugly bits, so we can learn different ways of seeing, understanding, and being in the world. When we know more about ourselves, we can be responsive to different attitudes, values, verbal cues, and body language. Particularly with autism, given the difficulty with theory of mind and communication, neurotypical people bear the imperative to recognize and function effectively with members of the autism community. Indeed, autism is a social group with a culture as worthy as any to expect to be treated respectfully for who they are (rather than ignored or denigrated for who they are not). This often requires humility.

Cultural humility comes before cultural competence and happens when people become "other" oriented instead of "me" oriented. It's about being open to learning about all people served by first responders and other professionals, rather than just the neurotypical majority. Cultural humility is also being able to acknowledge and accept the power dynamics. As unsavory as it might feel, it is important to recognize that the mainstream in any group has more power than those desiring to interact with it. (Often, mainstream people reject the notion of power, which is easy to do if you're the one who has it.) This requires an attitude of curiosity and a true appreciation for diversity.

Lisa shares:

> Living with autism is challenging. There are parts of being autistic that are more difficult than the rest. One particularly troublesome part is communicating my thoughts, feelings, and actions to others. It is disheartening because I am misunderstood most of the time. I constantly wrestle with how to say the right words, do the right thing, and get my heart in the right place to be the person I want to be, with, it seems, little success. My intentions are often misconstrued to be malicious and uncaring, when I try so hard to be just the opposite. My nature is to be considerate and kind, yet I feel like I have to constantly explain myself so others will understand my actions and motives, but I don't seem to get my point across. It's extremely frustrating because I feel that if my words can be taken as they are spoken, there would be little to no misunderstandings. I say what I mean and I mean what I say. The words I use have no hidden meaning and are not subtly twisted by me to mean something different than what I say. I wonder why non-autistic people don't use the right meaning of words.

The purpose of cultural competency is to increase the chances of positive outcomes and well-being of the people being served by helping professionals. It promotes mutual respect and awareness of the different ways people experience the same environment. Cultural competency is not only being aware of differences, however, but accepting them and working together so everyone feels respected and safe. Being culturally competent for an autistic client, for example, includes making compassionate accommodations when and where genuinely possible (rather than based on convenience) in consideration of someone else's sensory sensitivities.

Compromises might also include things like not having a big birthday celebration for an autistic child just because so many other children have one. The autistic child isn't like every other child; in fact, every other child isn't like the next one, regardless of their neurocognitive structure. It would be culturally sensitive, instead of assuming, to ask the child what they want, and do that, even it if seems small, quiet, and doesn't include a lot of people. It will mean so much more to the child to be understood than to have a big birthday bash. In this example, showing the child they are understood requires awareness (of what you, the caretaker, wants for the child as well as what the child might want for themselves), acceptance, and respect for the person being helped.

Practical skills for connecting with a myriad of different cultures

DO

- Listen carefully.

- Show your face and lips when speaking.

- Speak slowly.

- Speak clearly.

- Focus on the main points.

- Use words the other person uses.

- Write down words when spoken words aren't understood.

- Assume your lack of knowledge first.

- Know that you are capable of adapting, too.

- Keep judgments out; let wonder in.

DON'T

- Use words others might not know: dissuade yourself from hubris.

- Use slang, jargon, or abbreviation.

- Use contractions.

- Use words with a negative meaning such as "barely," "hardly," or "don't."

- Speak very fast, or with a mumble.

- Use stereotypes.

- Assume cultural competence is necessary only if you're in direct contact with people other than yourself.

- Make generalizations—that every person in a category reacts the same way.

To be sure, cultural competency is not a one-day training. It is a process of continual learning. It's a dedication to practicing. It will come with mistakes and misunderstandings. Keeping an open mind and being willing to listen to what autistic people are saying (rather than what you want them to be saying) are great steps towards cultural competency.

Lisa states:

What I've found out that is interesting to me, as previously stated, is that I follow social etiquette, try hard to make no social mistakes, and apologize for any social blunder I might make, only to experience the non-autistic people seeming to dismiss social etiquette, be rude, bully me, patronize me, ignore me, and blame the botched interaction on me simply because of my diagnosis of autism. It seems to be socially acceptable to blame me because I'm autistic instead of looking at their own behaviors in relation to what I'm telling them I need.

It's a lot of work for me to know what to say, when to say it, where to look, the right distance to stand away, how long to talk, how to begin a conversation, how to end a conversation, and to figure out what is really being said that everyone else except for me seems to understand. Then, on top of all that, I'm required to "not act autistic."

Practical skills for supporting ASD people

Keeping the basics of cultural competency in mind, here are some suggestions for how to support autistic people with PTSD on a daily basis:

- Go further than just being aware; acceptance is needed.

- Be willing to embrace differences instead of fearing and/ or rejecting them.

- Be aware of any propensity to patronize; presume we are competent.

- Be willing to explain NT behavior that autistic people don't understand and ask about autistic behavior NTs don't understand.

- Regarding sensory issues: when suggesting places to go, be aware of the environment for your autistic friend/co-worker/family member/client. Having empathy is helpful in any relationship.

- Regarding emotions: understand that autistic people will not feel or display emotions in the same way as NT people.

- Understand autistic people may need time alone or may decline an invitation(s) and it has nothing to do with the other person. If you want to be with your autistic friend, keep asking.

- Open communication: don't just end a relationship with an autistic person abruptly; be open and honest with them if they are doing something you don't like.

- Be aware of the often unconscious behavior of ableism; there's so much more to us than our "diff-abilities."

- Don't try to change autistic people into non-autistic people.

- Don't try to "cure" your friend or recommend any possible ways they may be cured.

In addition to the above, recognize that for ASD and other communication-challenged differences, silence isn't a disconnect; it's communicating in a different form. Many first responders and early-professional providers are uncomfortable with silence and try to fill in the voids, or pull information out of a patient. They often will barrage the person with questions; this is understandable because time is a critical issue and information is key to helping with diagnosis and treatment. Silence, though, is often an indicator that the autistic or traumatized person is overwhelmed. They freeze—flee on the inside. This is dangerous, because systems are feeling threatened, brain connections are misfiring, and stimulation is being misinterpreted. Often, these situations are re-traumatizing, no matter how well-meaning the helper. There will be more accurate information given and a better outcome if the helper can slow down just a little bit. Also, take the patient away from lights and sirens, close the door or leave it open, sit in silence and breathe. Though it seems antithetical, waiting can actually give you time.

Crisis response

When in a short-term, fast-paced, emergency-type situation, there are additional things of which to be aware. Here's what first responders should know:

- Recognize that the autistic patient may have no words; they may not be able to tell a first responder what they need.

- Do not touch if it isn't absolutely necessary; touch is not soothing.

- Do not force the autistic patient to pat a therapy dog; it may not help. Let the patient decide.

- Be aware of the ambient "noise" of the situation, such as bright lights, sirens, traffic, and machines.

- Allow the patient some time to answer; processing may be even slower when in crisis.

- Recognize that, regardless of how the autistic patient looks, they are likely in a state of extremely high anxiety.

- Listen to what they're saying: don't just listen for what you think you need to know.

- Talk to the autistic patient as you would any other person regarding their body, symptoms, and so on; only, wait a bit for the response. Do not barrage them with questions.

Lisa shares:

> I went on a tour through the Salem Witch museum with some family. While walking down some stairs, I missed a step. I fell and landed on my ankle the wrong way. I was in the middle of the crowd and people were walking around me not stopping to let me get out of the way. I managed to crawl

to the nearest wall. Someone told a museum employee. The director found her way to me and started asking questions. My ankle really hurt, some people circled me, watching what would happen, my sister was trying to talk to me, and my boys looked scared. I needed time. The director kept asking me if I could walk. I told her no, not realizing she was going to take action without telling me.

I was planning how to get out of there myself when a gurney and a couple of men came around the corner. I had no idea other people were deciding what was going to happen to me. The men with the gurney had one goal, to get me onto the stretcher and to the hospital. I did not want to go with those men. I was taken out of the museum without being able to tell my sons where I was going, how I felt, that there was no emergency, and how to get back to me. My sister couldn't go into the ambulance with me. Inside the ambulance, the siren was too loud. I was being poked and men were talking. No one had listened to me or given me any time to process what was happening. I didn't know where I was being taken. I didn't know where my kids were or if my sister really knew where I was going.

At the hospital, I was given an x-ray and then left in a corner to watch the craziness of people in the emergency room of a big hospital. I did not know what was happening as far as my care. I had a very long wait.

It would have taken two seconds for the director of the museum to kneel down and ask me what I needed, then provide me just that—which was simply, "a minute to get myself together" and "make a plan for myself." It would have taken less than a minute for the ambulance people to tell me what was pertinent to me, or the emergency room to let me read forms, and so on. I wasn't unconscious; I was fully aware of myself and I knew what I needed to do for myself, but I'd lost my power.

Chapter X

Finding a Helpful Therapeutic Approach

I. Review of models

Given the lack of research on the co-occurrence of ASD and PTSD, it stands to reason that there isn't any sort of proven or "best practice" model. What's more, a review of the literature on ASD alone reveals that the most research, by far, is done regarding children, adolescents, and young adults. At the present time, there is very little published on treating autism in mid-life and older adults, most of which discusses the paucity of information and need for evidence-based, quality models of treatment (e.g., Murphy *et al.* 2016). Thus, in the present case, it became necessary to look individually at treatment for PTSD then for ASD, and to find the overlap, if possible.

Treatment of PTSD

Looking at the guidelines for treating PTSD, researchers at Emory University found three therapeutic models recommended by both the CDC (Centers for Disease Control and Prevention) and the American Psychological Society (Watkins, Spring and Rothbaum 2018). These models are Prolonged Exposure Therapy (PE), Cognitive Processing Therapy (CPT), and Trauma Focused Cognitive Behavioral Therapy (TF-CBT; for children and adolescents). Treatment in general focused on addressing memories and feelings of the traumatic events.

PE is a technique expecting to change the fear structures in the brain. It involves helping the client to activate the fear center while at the same time learning and inputting new information that challenges the client's reality. Several studies have shown PE to be effective in decreasing trauma symptoms. There is also evidence that PE can work when co-occurring disorders (e.g., anxiety, depression).

Building on PE, CPT, also evidence-based, is meant to assist clients in recognizing distorted cognitions and how they impact their daily life (Resick, Monson and Chard 2016). Practitioners challenge ineffective cognitions that aren't reflected in the client's current environment. When successful, CPT helps people to shift reference points such that personal appraisals become more in line with real-world experiences.

Finally, in TF-CBT, clients are helped to explore alternative explanations to rigidly held beliefs (Cohen *et al.* 2000). Negative appraisals of the situation, and guilt that often exacerbates symptomology, are faced in a safe, accepting atmosphere. This form of treatment was developed for children and adolescents who have experienced traumas. It also involves their caregivers so that together they can learn about trauma and how to recognize intense emotions and maladaptive thoughts.

Treatment of ASD

In attempting to identify treatment guidelines for ASD, one would find few specific suggestions for chronologically mature clients. For the young, whose brains are still plastic and growing—and whose lives are (hopefully) surrounded by the systematic structures of school, community, and caretaker support—interventions are designed to increase skills for social interaction, communication, and cognitive or behavioral rigidity.

Best practice suggests individualized programming in natural settings with shared control and natural contingencies.

Applied Behavioral Analysis (ABA), which seeks to increase socially acceptable behaviors by linking them with the client's environment, has been thought of as a standard for training the young autistic minds. Many studies show an improvement in exhibiting preferred behaviors (e.g., Makrygianni, Gena, Katoudi and Galanis 2018). Other studies have suggested, however, that while ABA often improves desired behaviors, it is an intense program that has some major issues such as confusion with reinforcements, subjective understanding, and generalizing, to name a few (e.g., Milton 2018). It has also been proffered that ABA can lead to participants developing co-occurring symptoms such as anxiety, depression, and PTSD (Kupferstein 2018). Of note, however, is that research into the treatment for autism often relies on ideas that autism can be corrected and clients' behaviors can be helped to fit into mainstream, socially acceptable categories that rely on someone else's idea of "acceptable." While children are helped to perform the behavior, their brain differences generally mean that they neither understand the "why" nor have the ability to consistently generalize new behaviors into other situations.

More recently, stemming from ABA theory and developmental practice comes an intervention strategy called Naturalistic Developmental Behavioral Interventions (NDBI). This model, also developed for children and adolescents, is meant to take place in a natural environment, where client and therapist engage in shared control of the process, and natural contingencies are used as learning tools. The naturalistic environment is found to be more helpful because children are already familiar with much of the stimulation in their environment, or when they engage in learning, it happens in situations where most of their life takes place—outside of an office—in uncertain situations that can give clients exposure to learning while the fear parts of the brain are engaged. Patients tend to learn the "why" of a sought response, and therapists can learn their own "why" for that particular client. Remember, autism is not a generally routine disability; it results from a differently structured brain that interprets, perceives, and manages information not only uniquely, but uniquely in every different situation on every different day.

Cognitive Behavioral Therapy (CBT) is also suggested for treatment of ASD as it pertains to helping the client develop perspective taking (Schreibman *et al.* 2015). The client learns to reframe negative thoughts into more positive, forward-moving viewpoints. Further, research shows that CBT treatment to improve social skills can be efficacious. For example, in a small study of ASD patients with co-occurring anxiety, improvement in social skills occurred during treatment and continued to show improvement at post-treatment follow up (Maddox, Miyazaki and White 2017; van Steensel and Bogels 2015). Other studies on ASD and anxiety demonstrate similar results (e.g., Reaven *et al.* 2018).

Combined treatment

In choosing treatment for the present dual diagnosis of ASD and PTSD, it is important to consider that PTSD is an emotional disorder affecting brain function whereas ASD is a neurological difference in brain structure from birth. Thus, the problem is how to work with the biologically different structure that typically has trouble recognizing emotions and communicating needs but relies on logic from the thinking mind, while simultaneously treating emotional challenges and distorted cognitions that are often out of awareness.

So, how did Lisa and MaryD go about finding a helpful—or at the very least not a harmful—model when none exists? First, they decided which pieces of the individual models seemed most appropriate for Lisa's specific needs. They decided to address the fear structures, distorted cognitions, and negativistic mindset while acting together with shared control using Lisa's natural environment as her "petri dish." They would approach things from an experimental viewpoint attending to results as they happened. They went slowly and carefully, discovering necessary pieces in this specific case, starting from the very beginning, with language, which is not necessarily verbal.

II. Important components
Vocabulary
Subjective understanding of words can be a challenge as a term has a dictionary definition, a nuanced meaning depending on a specific situation, and can be distorted by unconscious fears.

MaryD writes:

> In trying to determine the best way to work with the fear structures of PTSD in an adult autistic person, it was important for me to first understand the individual organization of Lisa's perceptions. For example, in identifying goals for treatment, I needed to know what Lisa saw as a goal leading to success. One word, "well,": neither of us knew that such a common word would be so tricky. It sounded simple: "I want to deliver my speech well." In my non-autistic perspective, however, "well" meant that she was prepared, had appropriate notes, delivered the speech, it was favorably received, and maybe the attendees learned something. Lisa agreed, and that's what we practiced. After the fact, however, I learned that to Lisa, "well" also meant she didn't mess up a word, the audiovisual equipment worked, and she didn't become overwhelmed afterward and retreat. Though the speech was well received, Lisa saw it as a failure. Neither of us knew, until then, that a single word had so many levels for her.

Understanding vocabulary is more than being "on the same page," because one word can send the dyad in different directions. What a non-autistic person takes as a definition and what the autistic person thinks of as a definition can be vastly different, and subjectively so. And the autistic person may be unable to clarify, until after there's a problem, or unless someone asks specifically.

Listening

Listening should be simple. Mostly, people hear: there's noise, but not much particularly deep thought. But listening takes full attention and conscious awareness: extra brain power. This is because neurotypical brains can think much faster than a speaker can speak, so while it's waiting, the unaware brain goes other places. It happens in split seconds. The listener might think they know what the speaker will say next, plan a response, think about dinner, and so on.

MaryD writes:

> If Lisa is experiencing overwhelming feelings—meaning she's facing far too many sensory or cognitive experiences at the moment—but she looks and sounds good to me, meaning she masked well, how would I know? I had to learn to listen through the obvious. I learned to be silent and wait for her to tell me which bits were pertinent to her at that moment; she didn't always know, but she needed to be listened to. Her experience, meaning the tolerability of treatment for her, was really what mattered.

Listening is an important point because no type of helping/service is cut-and-dried; many situations are unique. However, some in the service industry learn to "stick to the manual." That's often a mandate for the job. For many autistic people, however, seeking services is wrought with anxiety and discomfort, by no small measure, due to lack of listening.

Lisa shares:

> After my husband died inside his car in our garage, he wasn't found for three to four days. It was very hot and humid, and awful on many levels. Still, after Paul was taken away, I needed to have his car removed. The car insurance person on the phone wouldn't give me any information, let alone start the process of moving the car away. She told me they wouldn't tow the car away without his permission. I think she was doing her job by the book, but wasn't looking at the situation as it was. Paul was dead; he wasn't giving permission for anything. The car was baking. The smell of decomposition was overpowering to me. It felt like the smell went to my soul. It also felt like it was all over me physically, seeping into my skin and saturating my clothes. The house couldn't be cleaned, lived in, or sold until the car left. The woman was doing her job, I knew, but was she? The more I tried to explain my situation, the more she bombarded me with questions, policies, and attitude. I couldn't understand. I wondered what language I should be using. It seemed so simple. Just listen to what I was saying. It took so much out of me. I was talking to her from inside the house, smelling things, feeling things, trying to problem-solve, worrying about my boys, grieving, not understanding, and feeling like I was getting nowhere. It took me days to recover from just that phone call, which would have been so much easier if someone had just listened to the situation instead of the stated problem.

Lisa's right, of course. Being present in the conversation, looking below the surface, and seeing the actual person speaking—listening to them—are skills adults pay to learn. And they're imperative when working in the helping fields.

Lisa states:

> In my mind, there is no double or hidden meaning to my
> words. I don't use subtext. I don't even understand "reading
> between the lines." I say what I mean and my words are literal.
> I have had people upset with me because they think I'm talking
> like they do, with perhaps a hidden meaning to their words,
> especially when I'm expected to display a certain emotion—but
> don't. I don't understand this, and I get discouraged.

Perception

Similarly, the perception of what causes trauma is just as
important to know, as it isn't always what it appears to be.

MaryD says:

> A young ASD friend of mine and his caregiver were involved
> in a pretty bad car crash. As one would imagine, that can
> be very traumatic for any person. The swerving, sound of
> bending metal and shattering glass, silence afterwards,
> smells, sirens...all the things a typical brain might focus on
> post-experience is where helpers often focus. My friend
> acted out, couldn't sleep, wouldn't eat, and was very
> interested in any silver car. We couldn't soothe him. He was
> verbal, but he couldn't find the words. We saw a horrific car
> crash; his interest was different from that. It took many days
> before we thought to look at things from his point of view,
> literally. We went to the car and immediately noticed his word
> cards in the back seat. Interestingly, once we got his cards
> back, his anxiety calmed considerably.
>
> His caretakers seeing and experiencing the world
> differently, combined with the boy's verbal disparities and
> our myopic assumptions, caused him days of despair. So,
> we started where he was, not where we wanted or expected

him to be. In theory, this seems simple. In practice, it's a whole other skill. Also, just as my friend's caretakers came to discover an alternative explanation for what we perceived, helping the autistic client with PTSD to do the same is an important piece of skill building.

Safety

Once Lisa and MaryD began to figure out the vocabulary disparity, they set about re-discussing goals. Unbeknownst to Lisa (read: alexithymia), she was experiencing high emotional reactivity. Before dealing with any past traumas, they had to lower her in-the-moment stress reactivity. They did this in part by focusing on sensory assaults in the immediate environment, so Lisa could feel physically safe. For Lisa, this translated to the more things she could count on in the therapy room, the more energy she'd have to work towards her goals. Things they've come to understand are:

- no candles or other fragrance

- the white noise machine, but no water fountain

- soft lighting

- consistent appointment times

- limiting the color green (when possible)

- no talking with waving hands or sudden gestures

- a "deal" such that when something sensory happens, Lisa feels able to say what she needs when she is able (if we know what to count on, she can focus more on skill-building).

Finally, as a means of mental safety, the consistency of continually re-assessing and reinforcing items already worked on is important because the ASD brain tends to compartmentalize, meaning learning isn't transferred from one specific situation to another. In addition, in PTSD, the brain is often so over-stressed that new information isn't always retained. The sense of bonding also doesn't stay with Lisa once she leaves the therapy room, so re-establishing is often necessary before she and MaryD tackle the next pieces. Lisa now knows she doesn't have to remember everything and is free to ask for review.

III. Developing and maintaining trust

After so many years working together, Lisa and MaryD have come to a process that is somewhat dynamic. Because there is no proven method of treating PTSD in autistic people, they developed a mutual acceptance of each other's known strengths and limits. Lisa understandably has significant trust issues; because MaryD comes from a primarily person-centered perspective, of which the main tenet is unconditional positive regard, Lisa was able to say what she wanted in the manner she knew how to say it—which sometimes was pretty direct—and she felt listened to. She also fact-checked some of MaryD's psycho-educational discussion, which was nothing personal, and was relieved to find MaryD wasn't defensive. Thus, Lisa was able to slowly find reasons to trust.

Other things they found that contribute to the trust/ability for Lisa are:

- being able to make small tests, that is, revealing smaller, less intense things as a means of gauging her helper's reaction

- the helper remembering what she's said from appointment to appointment

- the helper sharing personal bits of herself when appropriate

- the helper doing what she says she'll do, for example, sending things, calling people, and owning up to it when she doesn't

- using direct language, including emojis, avoiding vague language...and being open minded about what something might mean (e.g., "later").

Lisa also had to learn to trust herself because she constantly questions what she sees. This is a fairly consistent struggle, not least due to polarized thinking and also to cognitive rigidity: though something agreed upon might happen for many months in a row, when an unplanned change happens, those months disappear and rebuilding is necessary, though from a better standing. For Lisa to develop trust, she had to constantly question whether MaryD meant what she said or not. There wasn't much MaryD could do at this time, except to be genuine, breathe, and see what happened. *But*, they were able to discuss things and practice perspective-taking. Lisa needed time to figure it out, and it took time; not minutes, *time*.

Shared control

In addition to the sensory consistencies and unconditional positive regard initially experienced when treatment began, Lisa and MaryD began to establish other features that helped forge a degree of hope for learning and change. From the outset, they knew there was no well-trodden path, no specific direction other than forward (which sometimes looked like backward). Thus, they worked as a team, shoulder to shoulder. Lisa hoped to be seen as an equal, not to feel patronized or coddled. At the same time, the cooperative aspects of ASD often had her feeling more comfortable in being directed, which made MaryD very *un*comfortable. Sometimes, they left a session mutually stymied. But the trust was there. The acceptance for what they didn't know was mutual.

Interestingly, a natural aspect of their environment turned out to be quite helpful. Because they live in a small town, there was the opportunity to discuss things in the therapy room and practice/observe them in a naturalistic setting. For example, Lisa belonged to a group setting of people struggling with grief. MaryD was active in that aspect of the community. They were able to use this mutual understanding of that to help Lisa learn, re-work, teach, and hone social skills among non-autistic women of her age with similar losses.

They also strive for various forms of communication. Other than verbally, they also communicate with a white board, drawings, diagrams, charts, and written narrative as a means of trying to understand Lisa's feelings and to tell her story. They discuss natural contingencies that happen in the course of Lisa's day and examine them from various perspectives. As theory of mind is difficult for autistic individuals, this is tricky, and Lisa has sometimes used Venn diagrams. Transfer of learning is also difficult, so tweaking and reworking a theory for unique situations is imperative.

IV. Open communication

Open communication, meaning each person has the ability to speak freely, can be challenging because some things aren't easy to talk about (attributable to trauma, in this case) while the appropriate words aren't always within grasp (i.e., alexithymia, shutdown, or selective mutism). Also, many autistic clients have a background of failed helper relationships, and those old experiences creep up to complicate the current one. Still, in order to maintain trust and shared control, both Lisa and MaryD had to be ready to hear the truth, even if it was hard, even if it felt perhaps counter intuitive to share and observe. The rule was open, non-defensive, and non-judgmental communication. This has been particularly important in the current situation, due again to polarized thinking, the negative perceptive mindset, and inverted life training (to always be wrong, bad, or burdensome). Vocabulary, too, produced a conundrum as Lisa and MaryD's individual understanding of "open" was different: MaryD saw "open" as an equal opportunity to say what they needed to say and to process things together. Lisa took open to mean directly honest. Thus, this is an ongoing goal.

V. Processing therapy
Understanding time delays (processing)

In working with traumatic experiences, it's often helpful for the client to re-tell their story or put words on their experience. Narrating the trauma often brings a form of organization to what happened. Because shocking ordeals can rob someone of anything they ever thought they knew, telling can also help to identify strengths as well as things they might do differently as they move towards reclaiming a sense of self; it can assist people in forming a new normal that they construct in new awareness while facing fear and uncertainty. It's very hard work.

With autistic clients trying to manage PTSD, however, recounting experiences without outside help could be more detrimental because of common time delays in processing. For example, the feelings about the story might not come right away; they can come much later in the week after the therapy session. The client may not even recognize the feelings, but they'll show up in their thinking or behavior.

MaryD states:

> When I'm discussing things resulting from trauma with
> a client, like difficulty identifying choice, for example, I'm
> looking for communication, but not necessarily verbally.
> Verbal isn't always possible since traumatized clients often
> can't recognize their feelings in the moment. I'm looking for
> somatic issues, like a sore back or upset stomach. I'm looking
> to see if they suddenly become quiet, which means the
> mind is full of things they can't find words for but which are
> distressing. The narrative may indicate stacking up tasks to
> the point of becoming overwhelmed. Managing after-session
> is also important because the delayed processing comes into
> play. It's important to have a plan for this. It will save days of
> rumination.

Lisa states:

> A difficulty with therapy and even conversations in general,
> is that while talking I'm only able to concentrate on what the
> other person is saying so I can understand. When I'm asked
> questions, I answer truthfully and honestly in the moment.
> I find out after processing for two or three hours—the next
> day, even a couple of days later—my answer would have
> been different. It's when I do process that I usually have the
> breakthroughs, or more importantly, questions. I always have
> questions and I'm always left wondering what it would be like
> if I could ask them in the moment. So, in therapy or with other
> learning/medical environments, I have later questions about
> most every conversation, but life also happens and there
> are other new things that come up, so I arrive at my next
> appointment with a stack of questions that there's no way we
> can get through in an hour, so I prioritize.

Provider-day struggles

Lisa shares:

On many days, it feels like there's no hope. It feels like I'm alone in my struggles, needing solutions that are not there. I feel disconnected. I have to mask how I feel for my children, while feeling completely hopeless and alone. Suicide ideation comes as another struggle. My mind reminds me of how stuck I am and asks if I really want to continue struggling. I have to find the strength to move through the day, showing happiness and other mothering things to my children while my internal life is falling apart very quickly. I desperately need time alone, but I have to pay attention to the topics my kids want to talk about, which is too hard to do in the moment, but they deserve for me to try. Then, one of my kids might have a problem, and they need me to be "on" to help them. Internally, I'm losing the battle; externally I appear ok and handling everything, which just takes up more energy. This all costs a lot.

Once, on a difficult day, I got a second to myself, and caught up on reading the mail, only to find a bill that was way overdue. I immediately drove to the town hall, got ready to talk to people, to figure out what happened and how to fix it. Once there, I found out that while I was getting ready to speak at a conference, I missed the due date. I paid the bill and the fines. Then, I was triggered because I remembered the conference and I felt like a failure for missing the bill and not meeting my goal at the conference. I got home and the kids wanted to go throw a football around. I did so and very quickly threw out my back and hurt my neck. I'd realized I'd been in pain for quite some time, but had just been ignoring it.

Now I had to make supper. I'd forgotten to go shopping and didn't have anything easy to cook. I remembered my car was overdue for inspection, so I was nervous about driving it.

I was too tired. That is how the therapy days (and most days) go for me—either the same day or the next, when it's too late to ask questions or reach out for support. And I lay awake wondering what I forgot to do.

Another thing I want people to know is that demeanor and outward appearance are not what's going on inside *at all* sometimes. So, some days I leave looking distraught and I am; some days I went in distraught, felt better, but haven't quite changed my outward appearance yet; and sometimes I go in ok and I'm not ok when I leave because maybe I remembered something or I got triggered and I look ok. Here I'm just saying that my inside (my internal world) and my outward appearance are not in sync. The reason this is important is because some days I present ok, yet need help—and some days I look like I need help, but I'm ok. I can also compartmentalize so well that even if I'm very upset—if something funny is said or done—I will laugh. That laughter had nothing to do with how I felt before and/or after the laugh. It's not necessarily indicative of my feeling better.

Sometimes, when I don't have words, people will say, "Ok" and just move on. Just like that. *But*, because I don't have words, it doesn't mean there's nothing wrong. It means the exact opposite. I may not have words, but I have a whole heap of feelings I can't deal with well, and I can't say that. So, I feel alone, overwhelmed, and unsupported. This is why it's so important for me to maintain professional relationships for the long-term. I can't really explain this to everyone all the time and trust that they will understand this. Once someone does understand this, I need to keep them!

When I'm in a bad place (unmasked, too) and it's time for me to leave a provider's office, I want them to remember that I was in a rough place like that before I came, maybe for days. Also, for me, what helps the most is when the helper leaves a connection open to communicate later via text/email/phone.

> In those sorts of helping relationships, what helps me the most is to be very specific on when/how the connection takes place; in other words, that I can ask for (and will receive) a call back or I can text something without expecting return communication...just sort of an I-want-you-to-know message.

Change

Change is exceptionally difficult for the autistic client with PTSD. Things like knowing what to expect and having rituals aid in safety and a sense of personal control. When out-of-the-ordinary things or surprises come up, whether a scheduling conflict or a decor change, both symptomologies come into play—the one that can't process and know how to act in a novel situation, and the one that ignites fight, flight, or freeze. There are doubts about safety, communication, and control. All else may be put on hold until equilibrium returns somehow. Trust in what they knew must be reclaimed anew.

VI. Patient rights

Patients have fundamental rights when they seek out assistance from a helping professional. They have the right to meet as many professionals as they need to in choosing the right one for themselves. They have the right to ask about educational backgrounds, specialties, and other matters pertinent to the professional's level of expertise and reputation. Patients have the right to feel safe enough to share private concerns and difficulties without worrying if they will be hurt. Patients have the right to humane care and treatment with respect and consideration of their privacy.

Confidentiality during sessions is imperative to building trust. While most people in the helping professions are mandated reporters, patients have the right to know all the information about what will be reported, when, and the reasons why. A patient has the right to decide what to tell and what to keep to themselves.

A patient has the right to know their options about treatment and to choose without judgment or coercion. A patient has the right to not try a treatment, to change their mind about a treatment, to ask questions about a treatment, and to stop a treatment at any time. They have the right to know their own diagnosis, treatment plan, goals, and long-term expectations. A patient has the right to honest and objective feedback on how they are doing.

Autistic clients' rights

In addition to the above, autistic clients have supplemental needs. Because they must work within the mainstream, they are subjected to mainstream peculiarities. Thus...

- A non-neurotypical client, at the very least, has the right to be listened to about their own neurology.

- Autistic clients have the right to be treated as autistic—not neurotypical.

- Autistic clients have the right to clarify anything the helper doesn't understand (and should be made aware of such).

- In order for a helping professional to have the information they need to help, the autistic client must be understood for who they are, not as a neurotypical and not as a general ASD person. (Remember, when you meet one ASD person, you've met one ASD person.)

- An autistic client has the right to speak using bluntly honest words in their efforts to get help, without being seen as rude.

- The autistic client has the right to be spoken to in a direct manner, without nuances, metaphors, or other linguistic vagueness.

- An autistic client should have the right to communicate other than by mouth; for example, via writing, drawing, and so on.

- An autistic client has the right to be believed in any way they present themselves, instead of having to mask how they truly feel.

- An autistic client has the right to be in a place that is as sensory friendly as possible, or to bring what they need to feel comfortable where they are receiving treatment.

- An autistic client has the right to not make eye contact.

- An autistic client has the right to as much notice as possible to change.

- The autistic client has the right to speak with their helping professional about either recording the appointment, taking notes, having a summary of the appointment at the end which highlights the important takeaways from their time together, or whatever is needed to compensate for a slow processing speed, provided it is not harmful to either party.

Thoughts on presumed competence

Many autistic people feel that helpers often don't help. There seems to be a stigma around autism—like every autistic person acts like Dustin Hoffman's character in the movie *Rainman* (Levinson 1988). Autism is different in every single individual. What isn't different is how often ASD people experience ostracism due to being unlike the neurotypical majority. So many autistic adults experience discrimination based on presumption of incompetence. Imagine what could happen to ostracized people should the mainstream shift its own thinking towards presumed competence, instead.

Presumed competence is what we give to people who look and act like us (the mainstream of whatever society you live in) or maybe who have lots of letters after their name. It means we give people our assumption that they can think, learn, and understand. (Note: It does not mean "in the time and way that is convenient to me.") This is a vital concept for an inclusive society.

Indeed, social justice movements exist largely to expose and address discrimination, including towards differently abled individuals. They work to reduce stigma by helping us all to review and shift our personal expectations of others. Once that is in practice, we must recognize and remember that inclusion does not mean that people don't need various supports. Most any realistic person who sees themselves as their form of success will appreciate the support they've gotten from, still get from, and hopefully give to, others in their sphere. As many biographies indicate, when someone gets the right support they are capable of some incredible things. Moreover, people with the right support can teach others so much more about the flavor and color of life. Call it Pollyanna, but wouldn't it be great if we could presume we are all on par as humans, all with our own strengths and growth edges? Perhaps then, instead of denigrating difference and staying stuck, we could, as a people, move forward, supporting and accepting support, taking time to see and be seen, and requiring respect as we give it?

Conclusion

Hope for Health and Healing

Hope—the one tiny word that, in Greek mythology, takes on all the hurt, disease, and other pain in the world—can feel elusive for individuals with autism and PTSD. Indeed, many with ASD/PTSD report running low on hope often in the course of a day. It is a vague term, not precisely definable. Thus, asking an autistic person about hope, one might focus on specific incidences rather than indistinct generalities.

For Lisa, hope is fleeting. She writes:

When I manage to use a new skill, recognize a cognitive distortion, or overpower the negative thinking, I have hope. But the triggers come and come and come. For me, a trigger is something I'm not ready for; triggers happen three or four times a day and pile on day after day, with little processing time between them. Still, my hope is to process all of my stuff—to be able to recognize it and manage it—and give myself a carefree day.

Hope is more than just having a set of goals, however. It includes the ability to trust and a vision of the future. For many who have experienced debilitating betrayals of their world, trust and the idea of a future for themselves are foreign. The idea that the world will go on, however, can give purpose to many.

Lisa continues:

In reviewing my experiences for this book and other works in which I'm involved, I recognize that I want to help other autistic people. This book has forced me to walk down reluctant roads, addressing things no one should have to address. I don't want others to go through what I went through. If I can help in any way, that gives me hope. It's the most hope of all, I think.

I write and speak on subjects affecting myself and my contemporaries because, thankfully, I'm in a position to do it. I have those skills. People say I'm brave. I'm not sure if I'm brave or foolish; it takes so long to recoup my balance. I have a hope, though, of one day saying "no" in favor of myself—of taking care of myself first—so I can be strong for others and for the autism inclusion movement.

I can use what's happened to me to inform and encourage others, to show them ways to find or give help. When I began this journey, there was nothing for autistic adults; there isn't that much more now, but things are changing, I hope. I've pitched my ideas to many and been turned away more times than I can count. Fortunately, sometimes—like now maybe—I have a hard time quitting. Thanks to my partnership with the American Association for Suicidology, there is now a toolkit that helps crisis workers and first responders to communicate more effectively with autistic adults in crisis. I'm also currently leading a committee to develop a toolkit about suicide warning signs in autistic people. I continue to write and speak and, I hope, educate.

My sincerest hope, however, is to start a dialogue—a motivated curiosity—regarding ways to reach out and truly help autistic adults. There are so many of us! I want to be a voice for autistic adults, for the kids who will one day be adults, and for those who didn't make it.

Epilogue

MaryD writes:

> I've learned how to listen individually...to each person; listening is connecting. I've taken courses in listening, and I thought I was a pretty good listener overall. But the skill has been honed to a much greater degree, thanks to Lisa's willingness. I've improved my listening through actively observing (rather than just reading about) traits like literalness and vocabulary. For example, at one point, I wrote that Lisa could imagine people's pain. We had a discussion about this because, though I meant "imagine" in terms of trying to know something the other hasn't told you, Lisa interpreted "imagine" as if it meant delusional. Another time, when I told Lisa she was naturally empathetic, she took it out because she doesn't know for sure if it's "natural." Also, due to her prior abuse, she was averse to saying nice things about herself as it had been considered bragging in the past. I also had to learn how to ask questions in the right way. Asking imprecise questions, like "How was your weekend?", proved too vague for an "accurate" response. I've improved my professional skills in the therapy room, too, in that I've been able to review my thoughts, feelings, and actions in real time and make, I hope, better adjustments.
>
> We had to create a working environment where Lisa could feel safe enough to recognize or process misinterpretations,

while also feeling valued enough to teach me; the working environment also had to be dependable enough for each of us to communicate our individual needs specific to writing the book. We had clear rules for handling the ethical quandary of dual roles and checked in often. We chose specific places for specific roles. We discussed what needed to be discussed when it was appropriate.

For me, what I like most at this moment is that I have developed a better sense of myself. Collaborating in a dual role means extra plates in the air, leading without being in charge, learning with humility, recognizing and managing change potential, and taking care without caretaking. In short, I've been able to practice much of what I have always said I believed in but, maybe at times, didn't always attend to well. I certainly appreciate the knowledge, courage, and commitment of my writing partner; she kept me on track and held me accountable. On the occasions when I tacitly pulled something out of my hat, Lisa had me specify my thoughts. Hopefully, I know myself better. Hopefully, I'm better able to assist the ASD/PTSD population and their various helpers. Hopefully, inclusion will become the norm—through actions and personal values. Hopefully.

Lisa writes:

As I wrote more and more of my experiences, I didn't feel very good about myself. I had to accept that sharing my experiences was just going to be part of the process. MaryD would help me to look at the experiences a bit differently, so that was good. I learned she knew more about autism than I thought she did as the book progressed. It was encouraging to feel understood.

I have a better understanding of why I did what I did or felt what I felt at the time of a certain event. I'm told that this is an impressive beginning in processing some traumatic memories. I have a much better understanding of how ASD and PTSD smash up in my own life. I can recognize and understand whether I'm wrestling with an aspect of ASD or I've been triggered much better than I have ever been able to do before. I am able to offset some symptoms before they become too bad for me to handle alone.

Collaborating with a non-autistic person was often difficult, especially if we were writing about the same topic. Sometimes, MaryD would have a vision of where we were going, and I did not. This was frustrating for me...and I figuratively saw topics like this:

DO EST VI LE CE

I couldn't "see" the direction the book was taking; thus, it was hard to know what I was supposed to write about. This sincerely challenged my linear thinking. At other times, I knew what I wanted to say, but finding the words to describe it was challenging. I learned to take risks and "go for it," writing my thoughts and hoping they coincided. I felt as if there were times I wrote material that would be wasted because we might not be on the same page, but we were always able to use it or change it a little to use it elsewhere in the book.

So, I was a teammate in a true collaboration. We wrote as true equals. I also appreciate the "presumed competence" on MaryD's part as she didn't care-take me. I decided how to take care of myself at any specific time when writing triggering or emotionally difficult experiences. There was no "ableism," and that is always a relief. I'm better at recognizing the need for limits. I also have a greater trust as writing this book helped me to understand just how known I actually am by someone. Someone gets it. She gets it. I have hope that others can understand this dual diagnosis, too.

This project came about due to my being unable to

find information on autistic people with PTSD. Truly, there's nothing out there. Well, there's a lot of people calling for something, but not much actually happening that I could find to help me. I've felt in the dark for so long—I read online and visit at conferences, and I know that this darkness is so prevalent. Two years ago, I began thinking that maybe I could use my experiences to help others in similar situations. But I couldn't do it alone; I needed a professional who "got it."

I think this book could only have worked with MaryD, because of our unique personalities and mutual trust. I trusted her to hear my stories and not judge. I knew the book would be difficult to write at times, and MaryD would trust me enough to say what I needed to say. At the same time, she'd be there to validate me and remind me I still matter. I knew that with her professional knowledge and my lived experiences, we could write a book that could validate others and give them hope that someone might hear us. I'm hoping that professionals—all professionals from medical personnel to legal people to administrative staff and beyond—can take time to read it. Maybe the book will give them the chance to open up their thinking, review their values, and work towards inclusion. In this way, autistic people in general, and specifically those with PTSD, might finally gain relief, feel understood, and be accepted/invited/allowed to contribute as full members of a more forward-thinking society. Bam!

References

Angelone, R. (2017) *Autism and trauma*. Accessed on 19/02/2020 at
https://autismcitizen.org/autism-and-trauma

APA (American Psychiatric Association) (1980) *Diagnostic and Statistical
Manual of Mental Disorders* (3rd edn). Washington, DC: APA.

APA (1994) *Diagnostic and Statistical Manual of Mental Disorders* (4th edn).
Washington, DC: APA.

APA (2000) *Diagnostic and Statistical Manual of Mental Disorders* (4th edn,
text rev.). Washington, DC: APA.

APA (2013) *Diagnostic and Statistical Manual of Mental Disorders* (5th edn).
Washington, DC: APA.

Australian Bureau of Statistics (2007) *National Survey of Mental
Health and Wellbeing: Summary of Results, 2007*. Accessed on
13/05/2020 at https://www.abs.gov.au/AUSSTATS/abs@.nsf/
Lookup/4326.0Main+Features32007?OpenDocument

Ayers, M., Parr, J.R., Rodgers, J., Mason, D., Avery, L. and Flynn, D. (2018)
'A systematic review of quality of life of adults on the autism spectrum.'
Autism 22, 7, 774–783.

Baker, C. (2018) *Mental health statistics for England: Prevalence, services
and funding*. House of Commons Library. Accessed on 19/02/2020 at
https://researchbriefings.parliament.uk/ResearchBriefing/Summary/
SN06988#fullreport

Bancroft, L. (2002) *Why Does He Do That? Inside the Minds of Angry and
Controlling Men*. New York, NY: Berkley Books.

Bandelow, B. and Michaelis, S. (2015) 'Epidemiology of anxiety disorders in
the 21st century.' *Dialogues In Clinical Neuroscience 17*, 3, 327–335.

Bargiela, S., Steward, R. and Mandy, W. (2016) 'The experiences of
late-diagnosed women with autism spectrum conditions: An
investigation into the female autism phenotype.' *Journal of Autism and
Developmental Disorders 46*, 10, 3281–3294.

Benedict, C. (2018) *Basic human rights for self-development*. Accessed on
19/02/2020 at http://serenityonlinetherapy.com/basic-human-rights.
htm

Bennett, M.J. (2016) 'The importance of interviewing adults on the autism spectrum about their depression and suicidal ideation experiences.' *Journal of Autism and Developmental Disorders 46*, 1492.

Breuer, J. and Freud, S. (1957) *Studies on Hysteria*. Oxford: Basic Books.

Cam-Crosbie, L., Bradley, L., Shaw, R., Baron-Cohen, S. and Cassidy, S. (2019) '"People like me don't get support": Autistic adults' experiences of support and treatment for mental health difficulties, self-injury and suicidality.' *Autism 23*, 6, 1431–1441.

Center for Substance Abuse Treatment (US) (2014) 'Trauma-Informed Care in Behavioral Health Services.' *Treatment Improvement Protocol (TIP) Series, No. 57*. Rockville (MD): Substance Abuse and Mental Health Services. Accessed on 13/05/2020 at https://www.ncbi.nlm.nih.gov/books/NBK207203

Cheng, W., Rolls, E.T., Gu, H., Zhang, J. and Feng, J. (2015) 'Autism: Reduced connectivity between cortical areas involved in face expression, theory of mind, and the sense of self.' *Brain 138*, 5, 1382–1393.

Cohen, J.A., Mannarino, A.P., Berliner, L. and Deblinger, E. (2000) 'Trauma-focused cognitive behavioral therapy for children and adolescents: An empirical update.' *Journal of Interpersonal Violence 15*, 11, 1202–1223.

Cross, T.L., Bazron, B.J., Dennis, K.W. and Isaacs, M.R. (1989) *Towards a Culturally Competent System of Care. Volume I*. Washington, DC: Georgetown University Child Development Center, CASSP Technical Assistance Center. Accessed on 09/03/2020 at https://spu.edu/~/media/academics/school-of-education/Cultural%20Diversity/Towards%20a%20Culturally%20Competent%20System%20of%20Care%20Abridged.ashx

DeWeerdt, S. (2016) *Memory hub could underlie social cognitive quirks of autism*. Spectrum News. Accessed on 19/02/2020 at www.spectrumnews.org/news/memory-hub-underlie-social-cognitive-quirks-autism

Donahue, M. (2018) *Surviving Bullies and Mean Teens*. New York, NY: Enslow Publishing.

Felitti, V.J., Anda, R.F., Nordenberg, D., Williamson, D.F. *et al*. (1998) 'Relationship of childhood abuse and household dysfunction to many of the leading causes of death in adults: The Adverse Childhood Experiences (ACE) Study.' *American Journal of Preventive Medicine 14*, 4, 245–258.

Fuld, S. (2018) 'Autism spectrum disorder: The impact of stressful and traumatic life events and implications for clinical practice.' *Clinical Social Work Journal 46*, 210–219.

Galovsky, T.E. (2016) *The influence of PTSD on quality of Life*. National Center for PTSD. Accessed on 19/02/2020 at www.patientcare.va.gov/chaplain/clergytraining/docs/CCTP_Webinar_Influence_of_PTSD_on_QoL_SLides_101916.pdf

Gravitz, L. (2018) *At the intersection of autism and trauma.* Spectrum News. Accessed on 19/02/2020 at www.spectrumnews.org/features/deep-dive/intersection-autism-trauma

Ha, S., Sohn, I.J., Kim, N., Sim, H.J. and Cheon, K.A. (2015) 'Characteristics of brains in autism spectrum disorder: Structure, function and connectivity across the lifespan.' *Experimental Neurobiology 24,* 4, 273–284.

Haigh, S.M., Walsh, J.A., Mazefsky, C.A., Minshew, N.J. and Eack, S.M. (2018) 'Processing speed is impaired in adults with autism spectrum disorder, and relates to social communication abilities.' *Journal of Autism and Developmental Disorders 48,* 8, 2653–2662.

Haney, J.L. (2016) 'Autism, females, and the DSM-5: Gender bias in autism diagnosis.' *Social Work in Mental Health 14,* 4, 396–407.

Haruvi-Lamdan, N., Horesh, D. and Golan, O. (2018) 'PTSD and autism spectrum disorder: Comorbidity, gaps in research, and potential shared mechanisms.' *Psychological Trauma 10,* 3, 290–299.

Hoover, D.W. (2015) 'The effects of psychological trauma on children with autism spectrum disorders: A research review.' *Journal of Autism and Developmental Disorders 2,* 287–299.

Hughes, K., Bellis, M.A., Jones, L., Wood, S. *et al.* (2012) 'Prevalence and risk of violence against adults with disabilities: A systematic review and meta-analysis of observational studies.' *Lancet 28,* 379(9826), 1621– 1629.

Hull, L., Petrides, K.V., Allison, C., Smith, P. *et al.* (2017) '"Putting on my best normal": Social camouflaging in adults with autism spectrum conditions.' *Journal of Autism and Developmental Disorders 47,* 2519–2534.

Just, M.A., Cherkassky, V.L., Keller, T.A. and Minshew, N.J. (2004) 'Cortical activation and synchronization during sentence comprehension in high-functioning autism: Evidence of underconnectivity.' *Brain 127,* 1811–1821.

Kapp, S.K. (2018) 'Social support, well-being, and quality of life among individuals on the autism spectrum.' *Pediatrics 141,* S362–S368.

Keefe, T. (1984) 'The stresses of unemployment.' *Social Work 29,* 3, 264–268.

Kerns, C.M., Newschaffer, C.J. and Berkowitz, S.J. (2015) 'Traumatic childhood events and autism spectrum disorder.' *Journal of Autism Developmental Disorders 45,* 11, 3475–3486.

King, R. (2010) 'Complex posttraumatic stress disorder: Implications for individuals with autism spectrum disorder – Part I.' *Journal on Developmental Disabilities 16,* 3, 91–100.

King, R. and Desaulnier, C. (2011) 'Commentary: Complex post-traumatic stress disorder: Implications for individuals with autism spectrum disorders – Part II.' *Journal on Developmental Disabilities 17,* 1, 47–59.

Kupferstein, H. (2018) 'Evidence of increased PTSD symptoms in autistics exposed to applied behavior analysis.' *Advances in Autism 4,* 1, 19–29.

Levinson, B. (dir.) (1988) *Rainman*. MGM/UA.

MacPherson, G. (2018) *The Body Keeps the Score*. Luminary podcast, Episode 274, 12 March. Accessed on 09/03/2020 at https://luminarypodcasts.com/listen/guy-macpherson-phd-183/the-trauma-therapist-podcast-with-guy-macpherson-phd-inspiring-interviews-with-thought-leaders-in-the-field-of-trauma/episode-274-the-body-keeps-the-score-bessel-a-van-der-kolk-m-d/bc655844-4ac8-46a5-9b6b-e8c9a95c8319

Maddox, B.B., Miyazaki, Y. and White, S.W. (2017) 'Long-term effects of CBT on social impairment in adolescents with ASD.' *Journal of Autism Developmental Disorders 47*, 12, 3872–3882.

Makrygianni, M.K., Gena, A., Katoudi, S. and Galanis, P. (2018) 'The effectiveness of applied behavior analytic interventions for children with Autism Spectrum Disorder: A meta-analytic study.' *Research in Autism Spectrum Disorders 51*, 18–31.

Martinez, R. (2015) 'How PTSD nearly stole my life.' *Huffington Post*. Accessed on 19/02/2020 at www.huffpost.com/entry/ptsd-nearly-stole-my-life_n_564a4bf2e4b08cda348a290d

McManus, S., Bebbington, P., Jenkins. R. and Brugha, T. (eds.) (2016) Mental health and wellbeing in England: Adult Psychiatric Morbidity Survey 2014. Leeds: NHS Digital. Accessed on 13/05/2020 at https://files.digital.nhs.uk/pdf/q/3/mental_health_and_wellbeing_in_england_full_report.pdf

Milgram, S. (1963) 'Behavioral study of obedience.' *Journal of Abnormal and Social Psychology 67*, 371–378.

Mills, R. (2016) *Reflections on stress and autism*. National Autism Society. Accessed on 19/02/2020 at https://network.autism.org.uk/good-practice/evidence-base/reflections-stress-and-autism

Milton, D. (2018) *A critique of the use of Applied Behavioural Analysis (ABA): on behalf of the Neurodiversity Manifesto Steering Group*. University of Kent. Accessed on 19/02/2020 at https://kar.kent.ac.uk/69268

Minkoff, K. (2001) 'Developing standards of care for individuals with co-occurring psychiatric and substance use disorders.' *Psychiatric Services 52*, 5, 597–595.

Morgan, L. (2018a) 'Just how hard can easy be?' *Spectrum Women*. Accessed on 19/02/2020 at www.spectrumwomen.com/education/just-how-hard-can-easy-be-by-lisa-morgan

Morgan, L. (2018b) 'Living with suicide ideation.' *Spectrum Women*. Accessed on 19/02/2020 atwww.spectrumwomen.com/featured/living-with-suicide-ideation-by-lisa-morgan

Muller, R.T. (2019) 'Misdiagnosis is all too common for women with autism: Suffering through a misdiagnosis.' *Psychology Today*. Accessed on 19/02/2020 at www.psychologytoday.com/us/blog/talking-about-trauma/201905/misdiagnosis-is-all-too-common-women-autism

Murphy, C.M., Wilson, C.E., Robertson, D.M., Ecker, C. *et al.* (2016) 'Autism spectrum disorder in adults: Diagnosis, management, and health services development.' *Neuropsychiatric Disease and Treatment 12,* 1669–1686.

NCC-WCH (National Collaborating Centre for Women's and Children's Health) (UK) (2011) *Autism: Recognition, Referral and Diagnosis of Children and Young People on the Autism Spectrum.* NICE Clinical Guidelines, No. 128. London: RCOG Press. Accessed on 19/02/2020 at www.ncbi.nlm.nih.gov/books/NBK92978

NCCMH (National Collaborating Centre for Mental Health) (UK) (2005) *Post-Traumatic Stress Disorder: The Management of PTSD in Adults and Children in Primary and Secondary Care.* NICE Clinical Guidelines No. 26. Leicester: Gaskell. Accessed on 19/02/2020 at www.ncbi.nlm.nih.gov/books/NBK56506

Ohlsson Gotby, V., Lichtenstein, P., Långström, N. and Pettersson, E. (2018) 'Childhood neurodevelopmental disorders and risk of coercive sexual victimization in childhood and adolescence - a population-based prospective twin study.' *Journal of Child Psychology and Psychiatry 59,* 9, 957–965.

Olien, J. (2013) Loneliness is deadly. Accessed on 19/02/2020 at https://slate.com/technology/2013/08/dangers-of-loneliness-social-isolation-is-deadlier-than-obesity.html

Reaven, J., Moody, E. J., Grofer Klinger, L., Keefer, A. *et al.* (2018) 'Training clinicians to deliver group CBT to manage anxiety in youth with ASD: Results of a multisite trial.' *Journal of Consulting and Clinical Psychology 86,* 3, 205–217.

Resick, P., Monson, C. and Chard, K. (2016) *Cognitive Processing Therapy for PTSD: A Comprehensive Manual.* New York, NY: Guildford Press.

Sayed, S., Iacoviello, B.M. and Charney, D.S. (2015) 'Risk factors for the development of psychopathology following trauma.' *Current Psychiatry Reports 17,* 70.

Schreibman, L., Dawson, G., Stahmer, A. C., Landa, R. *et al.* (2015) 'Naturalistic developmental behavioral interventions: Empirically validated treatments for autism spectrum disorder.' *Journal of Autism and Developmental Disorders 45,* 8, 2411–2428.

Stavropoulos, K.K., Bolorian, Y. and Blacher, J. (2018) 'Differential diagnosis of autism spectrum disorder and post-traumatic stress disorder: Two clinical cases.' *Journal of Clinical Medicine 7,* 4, 71.

Thompson, B.N. (2017) *Theory of mind: Understanding Others in a Social World.* Psychology Today. Accessed on 20/02/2020 at www.psychologytoday.com/us/blog/socioemotional-success/201707/theory-mind-understanding-others-in-social-world

U.S. Department of Education (2016) *Student Reports of Bullying: Results from the 2015 School Crime Supplement to the National Crime Victim Survey.* Accessed on 20/02/2020 at https://nces.ed.gov/pubs2017/2017015.pdf

U.S. Department of Veterans Affairs (2019) *How common is PTSD in adults?* Accessed on 09/03/2020 at www.ptsd.va.gov/understand/common/common_adults.asp

van der Kolk, B. in MacPherson, G. (2018, March 12) Luminary Postcasts, Episode 274: The Body Keeps the Score. Accessed on 15/05/2020 at https://luminarypodcasts.com/listen/guy-macpherson-phd-183/the-trauma-therapist-podcast-with-guy-macpherson-phd-inspiring-interviews-with-thought-leaders-in-the-field-of-trauma/episode-274-the-body-keeps-the-score-bessel-a-van-der-kolk-m-d/bc655844-4ac8-46a5-9b6b-e8c9a95c8319.

Van Steensel, F.J.A. and Bogels, S.M. (2015) 'CBT for anxiety disorders in children with and without autism spectrum disorders.' *Journal of Consulting and Clinical Psychology 83*, 3, 512–523.

Vranić, A., Jelić, M. and Tonković, M. (2018) 'Functions of autobiographical memory in younger and older adults.' *Frontiers in Psychology 9*, 219.

Watkins, L.E., Spring, K.R. and Rothbaum, B.O. (2018) 'Treating PTSD: A review of evidence-based psychotherapy interventions.' *Frontiers in Behavioral Neuroscience 12*, 258.

Wechsler, D. (2008) *Wechsler Adult Intelligence Scale* (4th edn). San Antonio, TX: Pearson.

Weiner, L., Flin, A., Causin, J.B., Weibel, S. and Bertschy, G. (2019) 'A case study of suicidality presenting as a restricted interest in autism spectrum disorder.' *BMC Psychiatry 19*, 1, 126. doi:10.1186/s12888-019-2122-7

Weiss, B., Garvert, D.W. and Cloitre, M. (2015) 'PTSD and trauma-related difficulties in sexual minority women: The impact of perceived social support.' *Journal of Traumatic Stress 28*, 6, 563–571.

Weiss, J.A. and Fardella, M.A. (2018) 'Victimization and perpetration experiences of adults with autism.' *Frontiers in Psychiatry 9*, 203.

Wong, C., Odom, S.L., Hume, K.A., Cox, A.S. *et al.* (2015) 'Evidence-based practices for children, youth, and young adults with autism spectrum disorder: A comprehensive review.' *Journal of Autism Developmental Disorders 45*, 7, 1951–1966.

World Health Organization (WHO) (2019) *Autism Spectrum Disorders.* Accessed on 13/05/2020 at https://www.who.int/news-room/fact-sheets/detail/autism-spectrum-disorders

About the Authors

Lisa Morgan, M.Ed., is a Certified Autism Specialist (CAS) and holds a Master's degree in the Art of Teaching in Special Education. She has previously authored *Living Through Suicide Loss with Autism Spectrum Disorder (ASD)* and is a senior editor for the *Spectrum Women* online magazine. She is also Co-Chair of the Autism and Suicide committee of the American Association of Suicidology (AAS).

Mary P. Donahue, Ph.D., is a psychologist specializing in trauma and loss and working in private practice. She is a collaborator for The Center for Grieving Children and has developed specialised 'Providing a Safe Shoulder' training for helpers wishing to assist victims of domestic abuse. She has previously authored *Surviving Bullies and Mean Teens, Coping When a Parent Has a Disability* and *All You Need to Know about Domestic Violence*.

Subject Index

Author Index